PROFESSOR CHOCOLATE
PRESENTS...

THE ULTIMATE GUIDE
TO FINDING
CHOCOLATE
IN NYC

Lower Manhattan and Brooklyn
Chocolate Tours

First published by
Chocological Publishing
200 E 16th Street
New York, NY 10003

Printed by Lightning Source
ISBN 978-0-9844580-0-4
First Edition
2 4 6 8 10 9 7 5 3 1

Publisher's Note:
Please note that we have made
every effort to ensure accuracy
at the time of publication. It is
always best to check that the
information is still up-to-date.
If incorrect information is found,
please contact Rob and Neill at
professorchocolate@mac.com and
we will gladly modify the text.

The authors, editors, and publisher
cannot be held responsible for
the experiences of readers while
touring. Your safety is important
to us. Stay alert and be aware of
your surroundings at all times.

Descriptions of the shops in
this guide are based on the
observations of the authors.
No remuneration of any kind
was exchanged for any profile.

Credits:
Cover design and photo by
Rebecca Shotz, rebeccashotz.com

Interior design by Maura Gottstein,
handpaintedinbrooklyn.com

Interior design and
chapter illustrations © 2010
Kurt Jeske, k.satellitegrp.com

Ordering Information:
Special discounts are available on
quantity purchases by chocolate
shops, bookstores, corporations,
associations, and others.
For details, contact the publisher at:

sam@chocological.com

THIS BOOK IS DEDICATED TO

GRANDMA ROSE
AND
POP-POP SAM

A NOTE FROM
THE PROFESSORS

One might say this guidebook represents a collective destiny that we started fulfilling as children. Though we did not meet one another until we started teaching in our early twenties, our childhoods are filled with similar toothsome memories. Each of us can remember raiding our family supplies of Russell Stover's or Whitman's Chocolate with total disregard for anyone else who might have wanted to enjoy them. Not only did we inconsiderately devour as many of those chocolates as we could, we would gently press the tops of the compact morsels so that their fillings would break through the outer chocolate coating. It was a method the young professors deployed to discover whether or not said fillings were worthy of our pursuit. This practice would be relatively harmless if one were to consume the damaged pieces of chocolate afterwards, but more often than not (much to the dismay of our family members) certain pressed chocolates were left to whither away in their little crumpled wrappers. Thankfully, our methods of chocolate consumption have evolved since those early days of experimentation, but our exuberance for this most wondrous of foods has only deepened. This book is a celebration of our enthusiasm for chocolate. It is an enthusiasm significant enough that we feel the need to share it with as many people as possible. We are, if you will, your personal tour guides through the vast web of New York City chocolate.

TABLE OF CONTENTS

INTRODUCTION

Between 15 degrees north and south of the equator, cacao pods are grown and harvested from the most sacred of trees. The gifts of these pods are the cacao beans, from which the beloved food we have all come to know as "chocolate" is made. The tree and its wondrous beans caught the attention of the 18th century Swedish naturalist, Carl Linnaeus, who busily categorized much of the known living world according to his binomial naming system. *Theobroma Cacao* was the official name bestowed upon the "chocolate tree."

While Linnaeus helped with the name, it was the likes of the Olmec, Mayans, and Aztecs who are responsible for putting chocolate on the map. In more recent times, the work of pioneers like Nestlé, Lindt, Hershey, Cadbury, Neuhaus, and others helped put chocolate into the welcoming hands of consumers. Recent estimates approximate the worldwide chocolate industry to be a $70 billion/year business. If other people buy and eat as much as we do, then we believe these figures to be accurate if not understated!

For the past ten years, we have been on a chocolate-finding mission. With so much chocolate in the world, and so many little shops here and there (especially in our beloved New York City), Professor Chocolate wishes to maximize your New York City chocolate-touring experience. "Professor Chocolate" is actually two people who have developed and co-authored this guidebook. We are elementary school teachers by day and chocolate-seeking aficionados by night and weekend. We do not judge the quality of chocolate, nor do we consider ourselves connoisseurs in the traditional sense. We simply love chocolate, love finding it, and love sharing our research with anyone who is interested.

Most tour books that we've seen are saved for profiling whole countries or cities, and have minimal sections on where to find the best food and sweets. Not this tour book. We've specifically created this handbook to help make chocolate accessible to the confection-conscious traveler. This entire publication is dedicated to uncovering, profiling, and mapping every chocolate boutique in New York City based on geography.

Many cities boast a handful or two of some very talented chocolatiers and their shops. New York City, on the other hand, is blessed with enough chocolate boutiques that two books are needed! This is the first installment. We hope that as you read this book, you will write and scribble in it as well. Ample room is provided per location to chronicle and describe your own chocolate-tasting experience. There are so many different kinds of truffles, bonbons, bars, drinks and barks in the world of chocolate. It is almost impossible to know just how your taste buds will react, so don't hesitate to document your personal favorites! Comments can, and should of course, be shared with us on our website: professorchocolate.com. Let the journey be the reward.

Cocoatastically,
Professor Chocolate (a.k.a. Neill and Rob)

HOW TO USE THIS BOOK

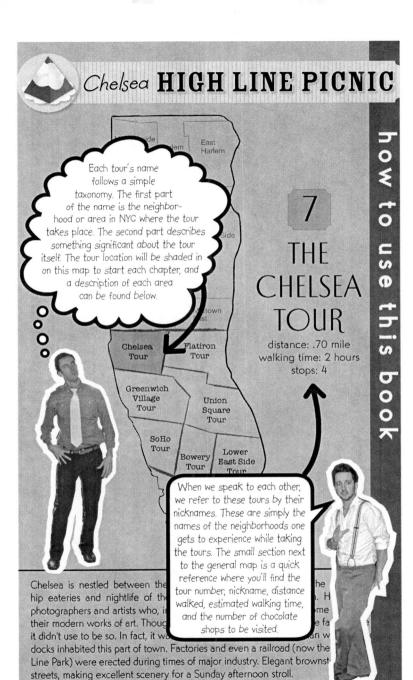

Chelsea HIGH LINE PICNIC

how to use this book

Each tour's name follows a simple taxonomy. The first part of the name is the neighborhood or area in NYC where the tour takes place. The second part describes something significant about the tour itself. The tour location will be shaded in on this map to start each chapter, and a description of each area can be found below.

7

THE CHELSEA TOUR

distance: .70 mile
walking time: 2 hours
stops: 4

East Harlem

Side

town st

Chelsea Tour

Flatiron Tour

Greenwich Village Tour

Union Square Tour

SoHo Tour

Bowery Tour

Lower East Side Tour

When we speak to each other, we refer to these tours by their nicknames. These are simply the names of the neighborhoods one gets to experience while taking the tours. The small section next to the general map is a quick reference where you'll find the tour number, nickname, distance walked, estimated walking time, and the number of chocolate shops to be visited.

Chelsea is nestled between the ... he hip eateries and nightlife of th ... . H photographers and artists who, i ... me their modern works of art. Thoug ... e fa it didn't use to be so. In fact, it wa ... an w docks inhabited this part of town. Factories and even a railroad (now the Line Park) were erected during times of major industry. Elegant brownst streets, making excellent scenery for a Sunday afternoon stroll.

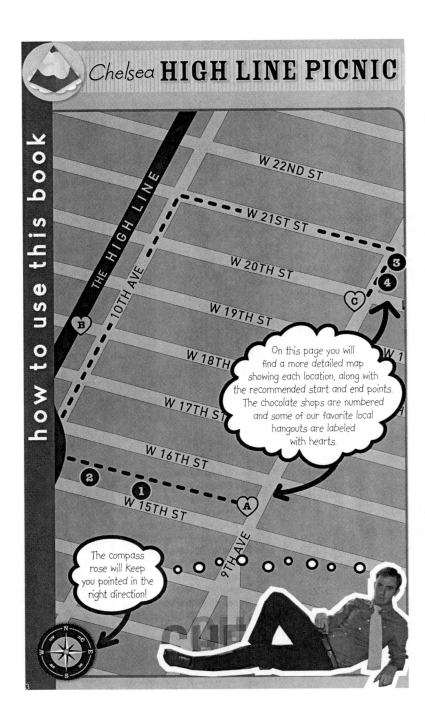

Chelsea **HIGH LINE PICNIC**

how to use this book

THE HIGH LINE

10TH AVE

W 22ND ST

W 21ST ST

W 20TH ST

W 19TH ST

W 18TH

W 17TH ST

W 16TH ST

W 15TH ST

9TH AVE

On this page you will find a more detailed map showing each location, along with the recommended start and end points. The chocolate shops are numbered and some of our favorite local hangouts are labeled with hearts.

The compass rose will keep you pointed in the right direction!

Chelsea HIGH LINE PICNIC

how to use this book

1 **Jacques Torres** (at Chelsea Market):
75 9th Avenue (between 9th and 10th Avenues)
This location at the Chelsea Market is like a dream within a dream.
There is a full selection of products at this location, including some
our favorites: Chocolate-covered Cheerios and Cornflakes.

2 **Chelsea Market Baskets:**
75 9th Avenue (In Chelsea Market near 10th Avenue)
Flooded with both natives and tourists, the Chelsea Market is one
New York's best places to forage for anything from chocolate and
sweets to meats and wine. The vintage architecture is a treat unto
CMB will help you keep it all together and share the experience w
anyone, anywhere in the country.

3 **Cocoa V Chocolat:**
174 9th Avenue (between 21st and 22nd Streets)
The northern-most shop on this tour, Cocoa V spe...izes in all ve
chocolates and treats. Serves breakfast, lunch, an... t.. as well.

4 **Three Tarts:**
164 9th Avenue (@ 20th Street)
The nickname given to three very talented women in past...y scho
stuck. Now they own their own boutique to show off all o... the ele
giftware and savory sweets.

> For the person who
> wants to eat now and read later,
> we've provided a quick description
> of each chocolate shop above and
> of each favorite local stop below.
> Each is listed with the addre...
> and cross street for
> easy navigation.

Chelsea LOCAL

A **Chelsea Market:**
75 9th Avenue (between 1...
Create your perfect picnic baske...
through this post-industrial theme pa...
with fine food stores and restaurants.

B **The High Line:**
Elevator access @ 14th and 16th Streets
(near 10th Avenue)
The High Line was originally constructed in the
'30s to lift dangerous freight trains off Manhattan's
streets. Completely redesigned and renovated, this
elevated park is now open to the public. A great
spot for a picnic.

C **La Bergamote Patisserie:**
169 9th Ave (@ 20th Street)
The fact that they are considered by some to have
the best croissants in the city only adds to the
appeal of its chocolate-infused pastries.

Chelsea **HIGH LINE PICNIC**

how to use this book

❸ Cocoa V Chocolat
174 9th Avenue
New York, NY 10011
212.242.3339
cocoav.com

CHOCOLATIER:
Patrick Coston

CHOCOLATE USED:
Organic, vegan, fair-trade beans
grown in the Dominican Republic
and processed in Switzerland

> We've dedicated two full pages to each chocolate shop. Above the icons you'll find information about who makes the chocolate, how to get there, when to go, and how to order if you can't go!

ry:

2006, Pamela Blackwell
d Blossom Restaurant & Cafe,
t restaurant specializing in vegan
. Three years later, she met a
d chocolatier who matched her
ant

> We've created a Key for you! To read a description of what each icon means, turn to page 11.

ey
he

V
otio
ean

Dominican Republic, sent to
rland for processing, and then
ded to the whimsical hands of
atier Patrick Coston. Above all
Cocoa V's all-vegan philosophy
sanal chocolates, handcrafted in
-site kitchen.

oston has had an illustrious ca-
at spans back and forth from San
o, Las Vegas, and New York.
Art & Design magazine recog-
him as one of America's top 10

pastry chefs in back-t- back years in
2002 and 2003.

Not only does C oa V create a
preciously-good line chocolate products, it also focus creation with
a conscience. Und ng the all-vegan
line of tasty treats precise execution to oid hurt ny animals during t ess aking the goods
old includes avoiding
dairy pr become common
practi for dairy cows to
be p imits to sustain a
stea leading to inhu-
mar a V eschews this
altoge nages to delight
our taste b

Experiei

Less th cks away from the
High Line ele k is a highly experienced pastry d chocolatier with a
truly unique Patrick Coston goes
above and b create a chocolates
that are hig alized, yet delectable.

5

HOURS:

(Seasonal)
Mon: 4pm—9pm
Tue—Wed: 12pm—9pm
Thurs: 12pm—10pm
Fri: 12:pm—10:30pm
Sat: 10:30am—10:30pm
Sun: 12pm—8pm

SUBWAYS:
A, C, E to 14th Street
C, E to 23rd Street

SHIPPIN
Year-rou   ng via FedEx an
              w
       ION

Below the icons, you can read
about the history of the shop,
the owner or chocolatier, and about the
experiences we've had in our travels.
In the "Professor Picks" box, we've listed
our personal recommendations for
each store as well.

how to use this book

Every treat in the shop is made onsite, never too far away from Coston and his staff.

According to their website, they are the first "100% vegan, organic, fair-trade chocolate shop to date" in the city. No dairy products here.

One of our favorite morsels here is the naturally sweet, yet not-too-sweet Agave bonbon, always on display and available on the website as well. A most delicious take-home treat is the Roasted Edamame Cluster, which is soaked in a velvety vegan chocolate.

Besides creating a unique and all-vegan stash, Cocoa V also serves small and inviting meals and snacks in a room adjacent to the displays of chocolate. This side of shop doubles as a lunche with enough seating for about 20. gan specials such as nut cheeses with wine, smoothies, and quiches out a very healthy and exciting The Professors frequently visit to the ever-expanding selection of some treats.

Chelsea **PROFESSOR PICKS**

May we suggest our favorites?
• Coffee Caramel Bonbons
• Roasted Edamame Clusters

Cocoa V Chocolat
Purchases

Truffles & Bonbons:

Name/Description: _____

_____

Rating: ☆☆☆☆☆

Name/Description: _____

We call this a handbook for a reason. On this page, you can keep track of purchases and give your own personal ratings for each one. Some stores have more than one hundred items to choose from! We gathered much of our data using pages like these in our own personal journals.

Rating: ☆☆☆☆☆

☆☆☆☆☆

Name/Description: _____

Rating: ☆☆☆☆☆

Bars & Barks:

Name/Description: _____

Name/Description: _____

Name/Description: _____

The Professors are very curious. We know what our favorites are, but we want to know yours as well. When we lead chocolate tours, we LOVE to see people's reactions as they enjoy their selections. If we can't be there with you, we want to hear about your experience! Please visit professorchocolate.com to share your ratings and experiences with us.

Name/Descr _____

Name/Descripti _____

Rating: ☆☆☆☆☆

Rating: ☆☆☆☆☆

how to use this book

7

Chelsea HIGH LINE PICNIC

Notes:

_____

_____

_____

_____

_____

_____

_____

_____

_____

_____

_____

> The world of chocolate in NYC is dynamic and ever-changing. We are looking for information to use when we revise and update this book as well as interesting material to include on our blog. We would love it if you would take a moment to tell us what you think!

how to use this book

Share your feedback with us @ professorchocolate.com

ICON EXPLANATION

 Facebook: Some shops have their own pages. We get updates about new chocolate products, store changes, and promotions through Facebook. Professor Chocolate has a fan page as well!

 Twitter: Staying current with news and events regarding chocolate shops is easier than ever with Twitter. Shops with this icon have their own accounts. The Professors lead free secret tours that we only announce through Twitter! Follow us, and look for those sweet tweets.

 Stroller Friendly: We've personally tested different tours to see how easy or hard it is to visit the stores when you have a stroller. We've even tested some shops using double strollers. If you are motivated enough, we're sure you can maneuver in and out of any of the locations.

 Shipping: Most shops offer shipping within the United States. This is the only criterion for earning this icon. We encourage you to call the shops that do not have this icon as shipping policies do change.

 Hot Chocolate/Coffee: If a location offers coffee, tea or cocoa (iced or hot), they earn the steaming cup icon in their icon bar. We enjoy drinking our chocolate almost as much as we enjoy eating it!

 Food: Some locations have a small selection of food items while others have sit-down service with full menus. Either way, they earn this icon. We simply can't resist sitting down for some food in-between chocolate tastings.

 Only in NYC: The 11 tours in this book include locations that range from international franchises to owner-operated, single-location shops. If a chocolatier or shop is based solely in NYC, they earn this icon.

 Wi-Fi: Most shops do not offer free Wi-Fi, but some do. Depending on which device you own, you may be able to legally access the Internet from a nearby source, but shops that provide it specifically for their patrons earn this icon.

 Seating: A number of locations have an area for you to sit and enjoy your purchases. Some have seating for large groups while others simply have seating for two. Either way, these shops earn this icon.

 Alcohol Served: Very few chocolate shops serve alcoholic beverages, but a great many people are interested in the ones that do. Shops earn this icon if they offer any alcoholic beverages.

 Ice Cream: More and more shops and stores are offering ice cream, gelato, or sorbet these days. If you love ice cream as much as we do, you'll be drawn to the locations with this icon in the bar.

Financial District **HISTORIC WALK**

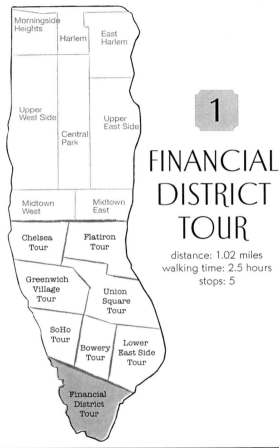

1

FINANCIAL DISTRICT TOUR

distance: 1.02 miles
walking time: 2.5 hours
stops: 5

Much of the heart of American civilization lies here in the Financial District of Manhattan. This district begins at the southern tip of Manhattan and extends roughly to City Hall at its northern edge. Currently, the Financial District is flooded with tourists snapping shots of the New York Stock Exchange. You are here, however, to wind your way around streets that have lasted for centuries and have seen their share of corporate takeovers and mergers. History buffs trot south from Wall Street (where a wall really did exist at one point to keep out Native Americans) to the tip of the island. This is the entire distance of New Amsterdam, circa 1650. Just imagine, less than 400 years ago, this section of the island was literally carved out by those ingenious Dutch. My, how far we've come.

HISTORIC WALK

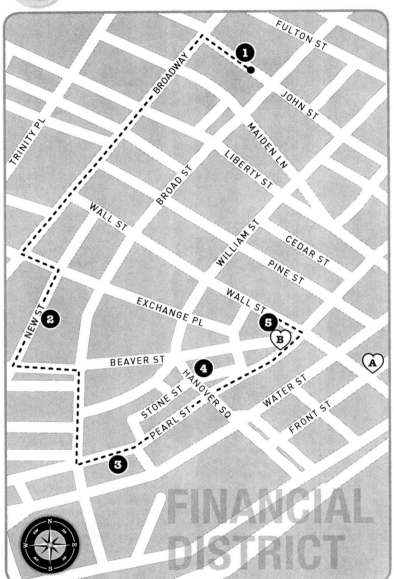

HISTORIC WALK

1 Evelyn's Chocolates:
29 John Street (between Broadway and Broad Street)
If you're seeking some old-fashioned, hand-dipped delights, then look no further. Evelyn's has been open for the last 80 years. Go in the morning when you might catch a glimpse of Evelyn herself.

2 Christopher Norman Chocolates:
60 New Street (between Beaver Street and Exchange Place)
Since 9/11, this shop has become a local favorite. All of the artisan chocolate found here is made on the premises. Don't overlook the artwork which is tastefully displayed both in the shop and on the chocolate as well.

3 FIKA espresso bar:
66 Pearl Street (@ Coenties Slip)
The flagship store boasts a 25-foot-long espresso bar and the work of one of the finest chocolate sculptors in the world. The Swedish craftsmanship inspired by fairy tales and magical stories will be sure to tickle your taste buds.

4 Leonidas and Manon Café:
3 Hanover Square (@ Stone Street extension)
For a traditional take on chocolate, visit these Belgian chocolate makers who have been in business for over 100 years. Take delight in some of their hearty morsels and their time-honored principles of quality.

5 La Maison du Chocolat:
63 Wall Street (between Pearl and Hanover Streets)
Fanciful chocolate exquisitely wrapped at this French institution will delight all senses. This is Parisian chocolate and elegance at its best. Free samples are usually quite conspicuous here.

A dark chocolate bar has 4 grams of the fat called oleic acid and more of a fat called stearic acid, which turns into oleic acid in our livers. This is the same same healthy fat found in olive oil!

Financial District LOCAL STOPS

A The Pizza Truck (literally):
On the corner of Wall and Front Streets.
Every bite of perfectly charred crust is crisp and delicious. Jianetto's Pizza Truck serves up some of our favorite in NYC.

B The Cocoa Exchange:
1 Wall Street Court (near Beaver and Pearl Streets)
As an official landmark in NYC, this building has significance in the history of chocolate. It was the site of the first cocoa futures market. It strongly resembles the Flatiron Building up on Fifth Avenue and 23rd Street.

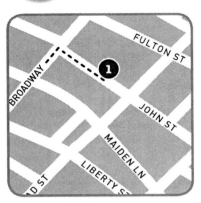

❶ Evelyn's Chocolates

29 John Street
New York, NY 10038
212.267.6178
evelynschocolates.com

CHOCOLATIER:
Evelyn Robb

History:

Make no mistake, Evelyn's Chocolates is a New York City institution. Evelyn Robb has been hand-dipping chocolate for well over 40 years, arriving early at 7:30am every day to prepare a variety of homespun favorites. It was Evelyn's father who first started a chocolate and candy shop along Beaver Street, only a few blocks south of the current location. Much later, the shop moved to 4 John Street where it proudly stood for the better part of four decades. The present location at 29 John Street has been occupied for only the last few years, but not much has changed in the family recipe book.

Evelyn's is the kind of place where familiar and friendly faces count. On a snowy winter day, we visited Evelyn's and found Alex, a congenial employee who was chatting with a regular. Apparently, this is a common occurrence at the store. Alex's warmth permeated the narrow shop, as if we stepped back in time to when storekeepers still lovingly talk to their prized customers. We were to later find out that Alex's mother also worked for Evelyn during the 1980's and did so for quite some time.

Evelyn's truly is a family business. It is one that has honored, and still honors, the age-old testament to remembering and cherishing their customer. It is no mistake that generations keep coming back to the tastes that bring joy to the heart, soul, and palate of every patron.

HISTORIC WALK

HOURS:
Mon—Fri: 7:30am—6:30pm
Sat and Sun: 11am—5pm

SUBWAYS:
A, C to Broadway/Nassau
J, Z, 2, 3 to Fulton Street

SHIPPING:
Shipping available worldwide

ADDITIONAL INFO:
Large sugar-free selection available

Experience:

Evelyn's is located in a unique part of the financial district where small businesses are widespread among towering buildings and hurried Wall Street workers. A small business Evelyn's may be, but the shop itself is as New York as Times Square, with a long and storied history. A place like Evelyn's stands the true test of time, almost as if it is a recipe handed down from one generation to the next. Both the old and young converge on Evelyn's, giving it a bit of a cult-like status.

The shop oozes with an almost domestic energy and the ever-present aroma of chocolate, making Evelyn's feel like a second home. Handwritten descriptions of tasty treats like Chocolate Coconut Clusters or Chocolate-Covered Oreos harkens one back to a time when life was just a bit more simple. Customers warmly converse with employees on a variety of topics, giving the store the feel of a worn-in winter coat.

The chocolate selection is old-fashioned, but oh-so-delectable. There are truffles to be tasted, but the heart and soul of Evelyn's certainly belongs to the variety of hand-dipped chocolate-covered morsels of anything hanging around.

Financial District
HISTORIC WALK

Evelyn's Chocolates
Purchases

Truffles & Bonbons:

Name/Description:

Rating: ☆☆☆☆☆

Name/Description:

Rating: ☆☆☆☆☆

Name/Description:

Rating: ☆☆☆☆☆

Name/Description:

Rating: ☆☆☆☆☆

Bars & Barks:

Name/Description:

Rating: ☆☆☆☆☆

Name/Description:

Rating: ☆☆☆☆☆

Name/Description:

Rating: ☆☆☆☆☆

Drinks & Others:

Name/Description:

Rating: ☆☆☆☆☆

Name/Description:

Rating: ☆☆☆☆☆

Financial District
HISTORIC WALK

Notes:

_____

_____

_____

_____

_____

_____

_____

_____

_____

_____

_____

_____

Share your feedback with us @ professorchocolate.com

HISTORIC WALK

Financial District

❷ Christopher Norman Chocolates

60 New Street
New York, NY 10004
212.402.1243
christophernormanchocolates.com

CHOCOLATIER:
John Down (a.k.a. Christopher Norman)

CHOCOLATE USED:
· Barry Callebaut
· Valrhona

History:

Christopher Norman Chocolates has been piquing the palates of foodies and chocoholics in the metropolitan area since 1994. After 9/11, the city dearly needed businesses to open up shop in the depressed Financial District. The gracious owners saddled up and moved from their Lower East Side spot to the current New Street location behind the Stock Exchange. Armed guards and their bomb-sniffing dogs can be seen casually walking up and down New Street alongside Wall Street execs. Fear not. These are some of the most luscious and sensory-essential chocolates made in the city; you're here to focus on these flavors.

Every bonbon and truffle is handmade on location with only all natural ingredients, guaranteeing that every morsel is fresh out of the kitchen. One of the proprietors/chocolatiers is John

Down, an energetic man very much interested in the process of creating a chocolate-art medium. Consumption of his hand-painted chocolates is quintessentially eating artwork. If you're lucky enough to get a tour of the kitchen, John will surely lead you to his prized paintings that adorn the adjacent lobby. The criss-crossing of both chocolate and art is a powerful and palpable experience at this one-of-a kind chocolate boutique.

Experience:

If you are unfamiliar with the tangled web of streets, alleys, and avenues that comprise the Financial District of New York, carefully follow the maps we have provided. When searching for New Street, which is more representative of a large alley, search for the unassuming. Approaching from the north, Christopher Norman is nestled in on

HOURS:
Mon—Fri: 8:30am—5:30pm
Weekends by appointment

SUBWAYS:
4, 5 to Bowling Green
J, Z to Broad Street
2, 3 to Wall Street

SHIPPING:
Orders placed before 2pm are shipped out the next day. Multiple shipping options including express service available.

the left-hand side of the pedestrians-only block and is anything but easily noticed.

Once you have stepped into this little slice of heaven, the high-octane energy of the Financial District is suddenly tamed. If you're like us, an immediate sense of tranquility will overwhelm your senses; take it in.

The chocolate morsels you see displayed range in flavor from very basic to most adventurous. Leaning toward the adventurous can be a palate-altering experience. You've come all this way, so be sure try something that can't be found in a box of heavily processed chocolates. Need help deciding? The Blue Cheese bonbons, al-

ways made fresh, are an eye-popping experience, and better than one's instincts would lead them to think. Continue to broaden your horizons with the Basil-Smoked Sea-Salt Olive Oil and Sweet Basil bonbons. A true connoisseur you are now.

Besides the variety of truffles and bonbons, Christopher Norman also offers hand-pulled espresso and coffee. We have seen many a customer stroll in for a mean cup of brew or a sweet concoction of White Hot Chocolate, foregoing the chocolates altogether. Occasionally, you will find a few savory pastries to the left of the chocolate bar display, always fresh and scrumptious.

 Financial District **PROFESSOR PICKS**
May we suggest our favorites?
• Blue Cheese and Dark Chocolate Truffles • Petits Fours
• Olive Oil-Based, Non-Dairy, Dark Chocolate Collection (vegan)

Christopher Norman Chocolates
Purchases

Truffles & Bonbons:

Name/Description:_____

_____ Rating: ☆☆☆☆☆

Name/Description:_____

_____ Rating: ☆☆☆☆☆

Name/Description:_____

_____ Rating: ☆☆☆☆☆

Name/Description:_____

_____ Rating: ☆☆☆☆☆

Bars & Barks:

Name/Description:_____

_____ Rating: ☆☆☆☆☆

Name/Description:_____

_____ Rating: ☆☆☆☆☆

Name/Description:_____

_____ Rating: ☆☆☆☆☆

Drinks & Others:

Name/Description:_____

_____ Rating: ☆☆☆☆☆

Name/Description:_____

_____ Rating: ☆☆☆☆☆

Notes:

Share your feedback with us @ professorchocolate.com

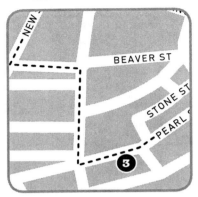

❸ FIKA espresso bar

66 Pearl Street
New York, NY 10004
646.649.5133
fikanyc.com

CHOCOLATIER:
Håkan Mårtensson

CHOCOLATE USED:
· Barry Callebaut

History:

Swedish culture loves coffee. So much so that they are one of the world's leading consumers of it. Leave it to Lars Akerlund and David Johansson to transplant their beloved home country's zest for coffee to New York. They opened the FIKA espresso bar in 2006, specializing in arabica beans flown in from a 100-year-old roaster in Sweden. Fika is a Swedish word that translates to "take a coffee break accompanied by something toothsome and yummy." We're not kidding! Enter FIKA Choklad.

One of Europe's best pastry chefs and chocolatiers, Håkan Mårtensson, was sourced from Sweden in 2008 to expand the FIKA menu to beyond sweets and coffee. Mårtensson holds the gold medal in the 2008 food olympics for his mastery of decorative chocolate. Drawing from fairy tales and a deep imagination, Mårtensson creates riveting chocolate sculptures with focused intensity.

Aside from chocolate sculptures, Mårtensson also handcrafts sumptuous truffles, bars, and pralines of many different colors, shapes, and names. All can now be found in three different Manhattan locations. The second shop, located in the Flatiron District, opened in 2008, while the FIKA flagship store opened up in the Financial District in early 2010.

Experience:

A few other FIKA locations can be found within Manhattan, but the Pearl Street venue is by far the largest and most comfortable, having the capacity to seat around 30 customers. Shiny white walls intermix with exposed brick to form a modern and minimalist atmosphere. On a recent

HISTORIC WALK

HOURS:
Mon—Fri: 7am—7pm
Sat and Sun: 10am—4pm

SUBWAYS:
4, 5 to Bowling Green
R to Whitehall Street
2, 3 to Wall Street

ADDITIONAL INFO:
Catering services available

visit, we slipped into our eco-friendly benches and a peaceful hour had passed before even thinking about leaving.

A full-line of fresh sandwiches and salads adorn the menu, along with delicate pastries and cookies. The special blend of coffee is roasted in Sweden and hand-pulled just for you on the glimmering 25-foot-long espresso bar. As tasty as these foods and drinks all are, the chocolate is crafted on-site by Håkan Mårtensson, the uber-talented chocolatier from Sweden.

Mårtensson will please any chocolate connoisseur with his ability to mix and match the hand-rolled bonbon flavors, (try the savory-packed Espresso bonbon for starters) but it is his world-renowned chocolate-sculptures that will certainly captivate. Even more exciting is the chocolate showroom where us gawkers can peek into the world of Mårtensson and his crafty sculptures.

Financial District PROFESSOR PICKS

May we suggest our favorites?
• Espresso Bonbons
• Gingerbread Truffles

Financial
District

HISTORIC WALK

FIKA espresso bar
Purchases

Truffles & Bonbons:

Name/Description:

Rating: ☆☆☆☆☆

Name/Description:

Rating: ☆☆☆☆☆

Name/Description:

Rating: ☆☆☆☆☆

Name/Description:

Rating: ☆☆☆☆☆

Bars & Barks:

Name/Description:

Rating: ☆☆☆☆☆

Name/Description:

Rating: ☆☆☆☆☆

Name/Description:

Rating: ☆☆☆☆☆

Drinks & Others:

Name/Description:

Rating: ☆☆☆☆☆

Name/Description:

Rating: ☆☆☆☆☆

Financial District

HISTORIC WALK

Notes:

Share your feedback with us @ professorchocolate.com

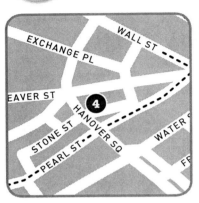

④ Leonidas and Manon Café

3 Hanover Square
New York, NY 10004
212.422.9600
leonidas.com

FOUNDER:
Leonidas Kestekides

HEAD CHOCOLATIER:
Claude Sénèque

History:

Just a little over 100 years ago, an adventurous American confectioner of Greek descent, Leonidas Kestekides, attended the 1910 and 1913 World Fairs in Brussels and Ghent respectively. In both years, Leonidas won awards for the best chocolate confection and quickly became a phenomenon. During his time overseas, he met a beautiful woman from Brussels who captured his heart and his desire to settle in Belgium.

Only a few decades had passed before the Leonidas name was spreading throughout Europe. The accessibility of fine chocolate was tempting to the palate of the early 20th century bourgeois. Eventually, his nephew, Basile, took over the family business and branded the company with the "King of Sparta" insignia in honor of his now-famous uncle.

Today, there are no relatives to officially carry the Leonidas torch. Fear not! The original principles set forth by Leonidas Kestekides have been carefully nurtured by capable and talented hands.

The Leonidas website boasts of the head chocolatier, Claude Sénèque, who travels the world in search of the finest ingredients. He more than lives up to the Leonidas name when it comes to quality and accessibility. In fact, there are over 1,400 outlets worldwide with well over 100 individual chocolates to pick from. Choose wisely.

Experience:

The Hanover Square Leonidas boutique is tucked in next to an Italian restaurant and only a few steps from an elegant, yet large, brownstone building named the India House. It's important to keep in mind that this part of the city does not use the grid system. Financial District streets run every which way and that, coupled with the towering skyscrapers, can become confusing. Be sure to follow the map provided.

HISTORIC WALK

HOURS:
Mon—Fri: 7am—6pm

ADDITIONAL INFO:
Vegetarian and vegan options available

SUBWAYS:
2, 3 to Wall Street
R to Whitehall Street/South Ferry

SHIPPING:
Shipping Monday through Friday with overnight and international service offered. Individual stores may have their own websites. We order from the Madison Avenue store online at leonidas-chocolate.com

Much like Hanover Square itself, this Leonidas location catches the first-time visitor with a bit of a surprise. Approach Hanover from any direction and it will seem as if you've found an urban pasture. The Leonidas store is marked with their signature navy blue sign.

As soon as you step inside, there is a display case holding close to 30 different truffles and pralines. Even to the most undiscerning taste bud, Belgian chocolate will be quite a standout compared to much of the chocolate showcased in this book. It is certainly worth your time to sample a few delectable, if not hearty, morsels of chocolate.

Belgian pralines, bonbons, and truffles are better known for their ro-

bust interiors of creams, fruits, and nuts. Think of these chocolates being gloriously matched with a cup of coffee and a fireplace on a brisk winter night. Sample the Manon Blanc, a white-chocolate casing that envelopes a cream dosing of coffee. Delicate they are not. Present at this location is the Manon Café, a coffee and baked-goods bar at the top of a raised platform in the back of the shop.

While there isn't an on-site chocolatier, the well-trained and very friendly employees more than compensate. There is also plenty of seating to enjoy your new-found love of Belgian chocolates with a cup of freshly brewed java.

Leonidas and Manon Café
Purchases

Truffles & Bonbons:

Name/Description:
_____
_____ Rating: ☆☆☆☆☆

Name/Description:
_____
_____ Rating: ☆☆☆☆☆

Name/Description:
_____
_____ Rating: ☆☆☆☆☆

Name/Description:
_____
_____ Rating: ☆☆☆☆☆

Bars & Barks:

Name/Description:
_____
_____ Rating: ☆☆☆☆☆

Name/Description:
_____
_____ Rating: ☆☆☆☆☆

Name/Description:
_____
_____ Rating: ☆☆☆☆☆

Drinks & Others:

Name/Description:
_____
_____ Rating: ☆☆☆☆☆

Name/Description:
_____
_____ Rating: ☆☆☆☆☆

HISTORIC WALK

Notes:

FRESH BELGIAN CHOCOLATES

COFFEE BAR
on the mezzanine

illy

Share your feedback with us @ professorchocolate.com

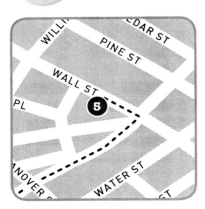

❺ La Maison Du Chocolat

63 Wall Street
New York, NY 10005
212.952.1123
lamaisonduchocolat.com

FOUNDER:
Robert Linxe

CHOCOLATE USED:
A special blend of cacao is custom made by Valhrona with a preference for Criollo bean origin.

History:

Walk into any of the four New York locations and it may not be so obvious that La Maison has deeply embedded and humble roots. In 1955, Robert Linxe, the so-called "Wizard of Ganache," began concocting truffles in a former Parisian wine cellar. For many years, Linxe struggled to keep out of the red by making chocolate into the wee hours of the night, so that customers could enjoy fresh truffles the following morning. As if things weren't tough enough, Paris was in the middle of social upheaval, creating much uncertainty for small-shop owners like Linxe. All in all, if it weren't for his talent and dedication, along with a wealthy father-in-law who believed in him, La Maison may not exist today.

In 1977, Linxe officially sold the business to Gaston Lenotre, but stayed on as its creative director until 2007. In those 30 years, Linxe remained a bit of an anomaly in the chocolate world. He was able to retain much of the creative powers despite a second buy out by Bongrain, a large French food conglomerate in the late '80s. Linxe was able to oversee and mold La Maison chocolates into the world's "gold standard of chocolate." Presently, the creative-mastermind position now belongs to Gilles Marchal.

La Maison's is headquartered in Paris, where all of the chocolate is closely monitored by a few talented chocolatiers who are dedicated to the principles of Linxe. There are a total of five locations in Paris. Two more are in London. One is in Tokyo, and four are in Manhattan. Those humble beginnings have certainly led to a prosperous present.

HISTORIC WALK

HOURS:
Mon—Fri: 9:30am—7pm
Sat: 10am—6pm

SUBWAYS:
2, 3 to Wall Street
J, Z to Broad Street

SHIPPING:
Worldwide shipping. Messenger service available in Manhattan. Next-day service available for orders placed before 3pm outside of Manhattan.

ADDITIONAL INFO:
Monthly newsletter available

Experience:

Entering into La Maison can be overwhelming at first, if only because of the quantity of white-gloved employees serving you samples of fine treats as if you were attending a cocktail party. There are a few other La Maison locations in Manhattan, and the only palpable difference is, well... the location. This is to say nothing of their chocolate or their chocolate products, which have been around for quite some time using only the purest ingredients.

Once you've entered this particular site, you will see that the periphery of the store is shelved and stocked with a substantial variety of chocolate treats delicately crafted in France. There is no shortage of elegance and refinement as everything is here is majestically packaged, certain to catch your eye.

The best treat in the store, however, remains their exquisite ganaches and pralines. Since there is no shortage of service, always feel free to ask for help and guidance.

La Maison Du Chocolat
Purchases

Truffles & Bonbons:

Name/Description:

Rating: ☆☆☆☆☆

Name/Description:

Rating: ☆☆☆☆☆

Name/Description:

Rating: ☆☆☆☆☆

Name/Description:

Rating: ☆☆☆☆☆

Bars & Barks:

Name/Description:

Rating: ☆☆☆☆☆

Name/Description:

Rating: ☆☆☆☆☆

Name/Description:

Rating: ☆☆☆☆☆

Drinks & Others:

Name/Description:

Rating: ☆☆☆☆☆

Name/Description:

Rating: ☆☆☆☆☆

Notes:

Share your feedback with us @ professorchocolate.com

2

SoHo
TOUR

distance: .75 mile
walking time: 2 hours
stops: 4

From north of Canal Street to the tip of Houston Street, with Broadway slicing through the middle, one can encounter some of the best shopping in Manhattan. Included in the deluge of these high-end shops are a few of the most charming chocolate boutiques the city has to offer. On your search for yummy chocolate morsels, you will cross paths with everyone from street vendors selling handbag knockoffs, to the sexiest people gracing our city. While here, if your appetite for chocolate has been satiated, stop by Boqueria (171 Spring Street between Thompson Street and West Broadway) for a freshly concocted batch of sangria.

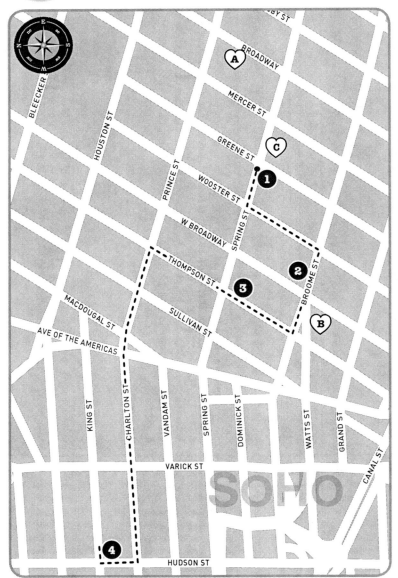

SoHo SWEET & SULTRY

1 Vosges Haut-Chocolat
132 Spring Street (@ Greene Street)
Katrina Markoff not only makes scintillating bites of exotic chocolate, but she's also concerned about the welfare of others. Vosges Haut-Chocolat donates to women's causes and is LEED Platinum certified.

2 MarieBelle
484 Broome Street (between W Broadway and Wooster Street)
More than anything, Lieberman has a flare for fashion and design. Nothing demonstrates this more than her exquisite SoHo shop and tantalizing decorative bonbons.

3 Kee's Chocolates
80 Thompson Street (@ Spring Street)
Former French Culinary Institute student Kee Ling Tong may create some of the most sought-after chocolate in the city. Visit early before the fresh daily-made selections sell out.

4 Jacques Torres Chocolate Haven
350 Hudson Street (@ King Street)
Mr. Chocolate himself is always on the go. He's opened four New York City locations in 10 years and a possible store slated for a 2010 opening in Dubai. Jacques Torres doesn't seem to be slowing down anytime soon.

SoHo LOCAL STOPS

> The bitterness of chocolate marks the presence of concentrated polyphenol antioxidants. This is twice the amount of antioxidants found in red wine and seven times what you'll get from green tea!

A Scholastic Store: *555 Broadway*
(between Prince and Spring Streets)
There are over 6,000 sq. ft. of books, games and educational software. Check out some of the store's weekly scheduled events.

B Ruben's Empanadas: *505 Broome Street*
(between Thompson and W Broadway)
Empanadas are Spanish and Portuguese stuffed breads or pastries, and Ruben's is our favorite place to get them. We've enjoyed brilliant blends of meats and spices as well as vegetarian options.

C Evolution: *120 Spring Sreet*
(between Greene and Mercer Streets)
The full selection of fossils, taxidermy animals, and other oddities makes this place a must see while you are in the area. We even took our students here on a field trip once!

SoHo SWEET & SULTRY

❶ Vosges Haut-Chocolat

132 Spring Street
New York, NY 10012
212.625.2929
vosgeschocolate.com

CHOCOLATIER:
Katrina Markoff

CHOCOLATE USED:
· Valhrona
· Felchin
· Belcolade

History:

In the late 1990s, Katrina Markoff began a journey that would later translate into a $12 million business, Woman of the Year award, multiple shops in the United States, and copious charitable donations. Markoff began her journey in France, where she attended the culinary school Le Cordon Bleu. At first, her interest in chocolate was minimal, but her feelings were altered quite rapidly after having an intoxicating experience with truffle beignets near the Vosges Mountains. So strong was her response that the mountain range became the shop's namesake.

Soon thereafter, Markoff was traveling the world in search of delicate and native flavors. Inspired by the food and women in these various countries, she brought her passions back to the States.

In addition to being the crea-

tor of exotic chocolate with a cornucopia of flavorings, Markoff is a strong advocate and vocal supporter of women's rights. During her acceptance speech for Woman of the Year, awarded by Women in Charge, the native Chicagoan shared stories about women who had been abused in far corners of the Earth, giving a voice to those that had little. Many were not only moved to tears, but were in total awe of a woman who, though highly successful, has remained as humble and authentic as one could be.

Experience:

If love of an idea or an object spawns collections, then Katrina Markoff is perhaps the queen of the chocolate collection. Dark, Milk, Italiano, Hip-Hop, Volcano Island, Marchesa, Gatsby, and Traditional are just a few of her majestic bonbon col-

SoHo SWEET & SULTRY

HOURS:
Open Daily 11am—8pm

SUBWAYS:
6 to Spring Street
C, E to Spring Street
N, R to Prince Street

SHIPPING:
Preferred shipping method is UPS.
In NYC, Chicago, and Las Vegas
same-day delivery is available.

ADDITIONAL INFO:
Chocolate of the Month club available

lections. One step into her store and you'll find the prodigious display of chocolate-infused products. This includes a counter of fresh truffles and bonbons which can leave you lingering for quite some time. We found ourselves attracted to Markoff's penchant for the art of eating, as displayed on nearby shelves. Shelves stocked full with canisters containing things like an elegant pancake mix that included chocolate infused with bacon.

Markoff loves to combine stories with the food she creates, so these are printed to complement each exotic truffle and collection. A sensory wheel (downloadable at vosgeschocolate. com/how_to_eat_chocolate) is a guide through the multi-sensory process of tasting. For those desiring the ultimate multi-sensory chocolate experience, Markoff offers workshops, retreats, and seminars.

Still hungry for more of the "Purple House" boutiques and website? Consider this: Markoff offers a purple points program through which you can earn yourself a trip to Paris by buying and eating her creations. Can world peace be achieved by consuming chocolate? After eating hers, we think maybe it can!

SoHo SWEET & SULTRY

Vosges Haut-Chocolat
Purchases

Truffles & Bonbons:

Name/Description:

Rating: ☆☆☆☆☆

Name/Description:

Rating: ☆☆☆☆☆

Name/Description:

Rating: ☆☆☆☆☆

Name/Description:

Rating: ☆☆☆☆☆

Bars & Barks:

Name/Description:

Rating: ☆☆☆☆☆

Name/Description:

Rating: ☆☆☆☆☆

Name/Description:

Rating: ☆☆☆☆☆

Drinks & Others:

Name/Description:

Rating: ☆☆☆☆☆

Name/Description:

Rating: ☆☆☆☆☆

SoHo SWEET & SULTRY

Notes:

Share your feedback with us @ professorchocolate.com

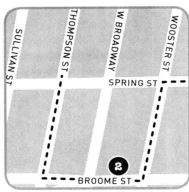

THOMPSON ST

W BROADWAY

WOOSTER ST

SULLIVAN ST

SPRING ST

❷

BROOME ST

❷ MarieBelle

484 Broome Street
New York, NY 10013
212.925.6999
mariebelle.com

CHOCOLATIER:
Maribel Lieberman

CHOCOLATE USED:
· Barry Callebaut

History:

Maribel Lieberman's knack for high fashion started before she began making her fashion-forward truffles. When Lieberman opened up her jewel-cased shop in 2000, she commissioned her talented husband to create paintings for her first line of chocolates. She silk-screened his colorful, abstract designs onto chocolate squares and designed a few herself, infusing them with savory flavors such as lemon, saffron and cardamom. Each of the 30 bonbons on the MarieBelle line is uniquely imprinted with one of these colorful and rich designs, mimetic of the complexity of flavor infused into the high-design morsels.

Lieberman's passion for art even shows up on her specialty '40s-style, pinup-girls chocolate bar wrapping paper. They are unique even by New York standards. She is noted once as saying that "art doesn't simply have to hang on walls." Art that can be unwrapped and eaten? We're sold.

MarieBelle's product line is quite extensive at both the SoHo shop and online as well. Her signature Aztec Hot Chocolate and packaged bonbon products have made their way to other fancy food spots in Brooklyn and Manhattan, making the brand quite ubiquitous.

Experience:

Upon entering MarieBelle, your olfactory senses are inundated with the sweet aroma of Maribel Lieberman's simmering Aztec Hot Chocolate. This frothy brew, along with other treats, can be found in the very back of the store. If you like café seating, proceed to this section of the store. Before you do though, contain yourself and soak in the distinctive vintage Parisian charm here in the

SoHo SWEET & SULTRY

HOURS:
Open Daily 11am—7pm

SUBWAYS:
1 to Canal Street
A, C, E, to Canal Street
N, R to Prince Street

SHIPPING:
Same-day delivery via messenger in
Manhattan. FedEx is the preferred
shipping method. Shipments go out
Monday through Thursday.

h

middle of SoHo. Antique mirrors and furniture house the full line of Marie-Belle chocolates, and they deserve your attention.

Vintage-style chocolate bar wrappers, hot chocolate containers, and gorgeously packaged bonbons greet you at every corner. Head to the main display counter that houses the 30 semiprecious jewels disguised as chocolate morsels. If you're boggled by the variety, you can always find a willing employee or fellow chocoholic nearby to help guide you.

Maribel Lieberman has not only created velvety chocolate and shimmery packaging, she has also risen to the top of the chocolate world with

the help of a dedicated staff. Her nephew, Rodolfo Espinal, has been with MarieBelle since the very beginning. If you ever have the chance to meet him, you, like us, will be swooned by his charm and warmth. On many occasions we have been the recipients of his generosity, not to mention inspired by his sense of fashion.

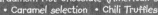

SoHo SWEET & SULTRY

MarieBelle
Purchases

Truffles & Bonbons:

Name/Description:

_____ Rating: ☆☆☆☆☆

Name/Description:

_____ Rating: ☆☆☆☆☆

Name/Description:

_____ Rating: ☆☆☆☆☆

Name/Description:

_____ Rating: ☆☆☆☆☆

Bars & Barks:

Name/Description:

_____ Rating: ☆☆☆☆☆

Name/Description:

_____ Rating: ☆☆☆☆☆

Name/Description:

_____ Rating: ☆☆☆☆☆

Drinks & Others:

Name/Description:

_____ Rating: ☆☆☆☆☆

Name/Description:

_____ Rating: ☆☆☆☆☆

SoHo SWEET & SULTRY

Notes:

Share your feedback with us @ professorchocolate.com

$\mathcal{S}o\mathcal{H}o$ **SWEET & SULTRY**

❸ Kee's Chocolates

80 Thompson Street
New York, NY 10012
212.334.3284
keeschocolates.com

CHOCOLATIER:
Kee Ling Tong

CHOCOLATE USED:
· Valhrona

History:

The charming and gracious Kee Ling Tong creates some of the more intense and exotic bonbons in the city. The ample supply of chocolate-mongers sometimes forms long lines outside her Thompson Street shop. This is simple proof that Kee's has carved a rabid following in a field filled with talented chocolatiers. In 2002, Kee Ling Tong left the business world and started a small flower shop, selling chocolates on the side. It was only a short time later that the dual-product shop transformed into solely selling chocolates. Using her expertise from the French Culinary Institute, Kee not only uses the finest ingredients but also always hand-rolls her truffles. They are never mass-produced.

Kee herself may be the first to tell you that her bonbons have thinner chocolate shells and a more intense filling compared to some others. This is due to the morsels being handmade in small batches and the use of rich flavors like thai chili or balsamic infusion. Even more impressive is the fact that Kee's does not advertise! Only by word of mouth do the throngs migrate to this nestled SoHo shop.

Experience:

"It was on a week-long trip to Amsterdam that I discovered the existence of small shops and boutiques dedicated to the selling and making of chocolate. I bought way too much, ate it all, and then went back the following day for more. Upon returning to the States, I decided that I'd like to find and visit all such shops in NYC. It is, after all, one of the premier culinary capitals of the world.

Not long after returning from Amsterdam, I arrived home from

SoHo SWEET & SULTRY

HOURS:
Mon—Fri: 9am—7pm
Sat and Sun: 11am—7pm

SUBWAYS:
C, E to Spring Street
N, R to Prince Street

SHIPPING:
Shipping is not available during the summer. Phone orders are shipped throughout the rest of the year. NYC courier service is available.

work and found that my wife had bought me a pastry from one of her favorite shops. I was beyond ecstatic. Along with this delicious gift, my wife informed me that she had stumbled upon another chocolate shop only several blocks away. I decided to investigate. When I found and entered the shoe-box size store, Kee herself was rolling truffles behind the counter. She greeted me warmly and proceeded to tell me about some of the pieces that she had on display. The moment I tasted the Almond Truffle for the first time, it made me stop and start to neurotically consider the question... 'WHAT ELSE have I been missing out on?' It is one of the founding inspirations for this book."
—Professor Chocolate

Do yourself a favor and don't miss out any longer. Everything here is delicately prepared and handmade with some of the best and most exotic ingredients on Earth. If you're feeling adventurous, sample the celebrated Champagne Truffle.

SoHo PROFESSOR PICKS
May we suggest our favorites?
• Almond Truffles
• Asian-style Parisian Macarons

SoHo SWEET & SULTRY

Kee's Chocolates
Purchases

Truffles & Bonbons:

Name/Description:

Rating: ☆☆☆☆☆

Name/Description:

Rating: ☆☆☆☆☆

Name/Description:

Rating: ☆☆☆☆☆

Name/Description:

Rating: ☆☆☆☆☆

Bars & Barks:

Name/Description:

Rating: ☆☆☆☆☆

Name/Description:

Rating: ☆☆☆☆☆

Name/Description:

Rating: ☆☆☆☆☆

Drinks & Others:

Name/Description:

Rating: ☆☆☆☆☆

Name/Description:

Rating: ☆☆☆☆☆

Notes:

Share your feedback with us @ professorchocolate.com

SoHo **SWEET & SULTRY**

KING S

CHARLTO

VANDAM

HUDSON

VARICK S

❹ Jacques Torres Chocolate Haven
350 Hudson Street
New York, NY 10014
212.414.2462
mrchocolate.com

CHOCOLATIER:
Jacques Torres

CHOCOLATE USED:
Jacques is one of the few chocolatiers who can produce much of his own chocolate from the bean. He even uses fully restored vintage equipment.

History:

Though he is officially known as Mr. Chocolate, and unofficially as the Willy Wonka of Manhattan, Jacques Torres is a renaissance man of sorts.

For starters, aside from being a world-class chocolatier, Torres stashes a 39-foot yacht at the Liberty State Marina, where he soaks in the Manhattan skyline and iridescent sunsets. The boat, much like Mr. Chocolate himself, doesn't stay anchored for long. Torres' passion (besides making chocolate) is to fish around Manhattan and Long Island with close friends, in search of his next meal. Keeping a third of his clothes on the boat, another third at a midtown apartment, and the remainder at the Hudson Street factory, helps keep Torres on the go.

In the early '80s, Torres learned the pastry trade from notable French masters. Not many years passed before Torres was invited to become the head pastry chef at Manhattan's prestigious Le Cirque, where the owners had recently built a custom-made pastry kitchen. Some time later, Torres opened up his first chocolate shop along Water Street in D.U.M.B.O., Brooklyn. The Chocolate Haven along Hudson Street didn't come until much later.

Haven is not only the gem, but the nerve-center for Torres' chocolate kingdom. With 115 tons of chocolate per year coming in and getting transformed into savory treats, the glass-enclosed factory gives visitors a first-hand look at the master performing his magic.

Experience:

Jacques Torres' Hudson Street shop could just as easily be called Chocolate Heaven. Besides a plethora of products like Chocolate-cov-

SoHo SWEET & SULTRY

HOURS:
Mon—Sat: 9am—7pm
Sun: 10am—6pm

SUBWAYS:
1 to Houston Street
C, E to Spring Street

SHIPPING:
Year-round shipping with FedEx.
Monday through Thursday overnight
available.

ADDITIONAL INFO:
Chocolate of the Month Club available

ered Cheerios and chunky-chocolaty cookies, Torres has also created his own ice cream line. Sample you must! Torres, never camera-shy, invites us all to observe and learn how chocolate is created from cocoao beans on Hudson Street. This is one of the few places in New York City where you can actually see chocolate fructifying before your eyes. It's truly an art form unto itself. The memory of the smell alone is enough to make us dream about being there, and it's absolutely worth the visit.

One of the first times we ventured into Chocolate Haven, we sampled nine different truffles. They were all scrumptious in their own right. Perhaps the real treat was salivating over the chocolate-coating machine, overseen by Torres himself at the time. So enthralled were we that we decided to bring home bags of Chocolate-covered Cornflakes and Cheerios. Our purchases represented just a few pieces out of the 25,000 made daily. Endearing us to Mr. Torres even more is his ability to use a hands-on approach in his business and still continue to expand his chocolate kingdom. He's mastered doing this without losing the integrity and taste of his glorious chocolate.

SoHo PROFESSOR PICKS

May we suggest our favorites?
• Chocolate-covered Cheerios & Cornflakes
• Hot Chocolate (made with real chocolate, not cocoa powder)
• Almondine Truffles

SoHo SWEET & SULTRY

Jacques Torres Chocolate Haven Purchases

Truffles & Bonbons:

Name/Description:

Rating: ☆☆☆☆☆

Name/Description:

Rating: ☆☆☆☆☆

Name/Description:

Rating: ☆☆☆☆☆

Name/Description:

Rating: ☆☆☆☆☆

Bars & Barks:

Name/Description:

Rating: ☆☆☆☆☆

Name/Description:

Rating: ☆☆☆☆☆

Name/Description:

Rating: ☆☆☆☆☆

Drinks & Others:

Name/Description:

Rating: ☆☆☆☆☆

Name/Description:

Rating: ☆☆☆☆☆

SoHo SWEET & SULTRY

Notes:

_____

_____

_____

_____

_____

_____

_____

_____

_____

_____

_____

_____

_____

Share your feedback with us @ professorchocolate.com

The Bowery XOCOATL FOOTPATH

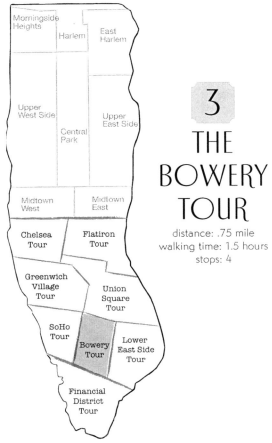

3

THE BOWERY TOUR

distance: .75 mile
walking time: 1.5 hours
stops: 4

Having once been a Lenape footpath that stretched the length of Manhattan, the Bowery, now located in the southern portion of the island, has seen an uptick in gentrification the last few years. The Bowery is encased by E 4th Street to the north and Canal Street to the south. Bowery and Allen Street enclose the western and eastern borders respectively. The Bowery's recent revival is mainly due to shimmering new condo buildings, swanky modern art museums, and even a Whole Foods (as featured on this tour). Not always has the Bowery been the center of such upscale construction. Its history is riddled with everything from Dutch farms to copious brothels to the dank and dark days of when the Third Avenue El railed overhead. Lingering still is a healthy amount of residual edginess, intermixed with the new and modern. (For more information on the meaning of "xocoatl" visit our blog @ professorchocolate.com).

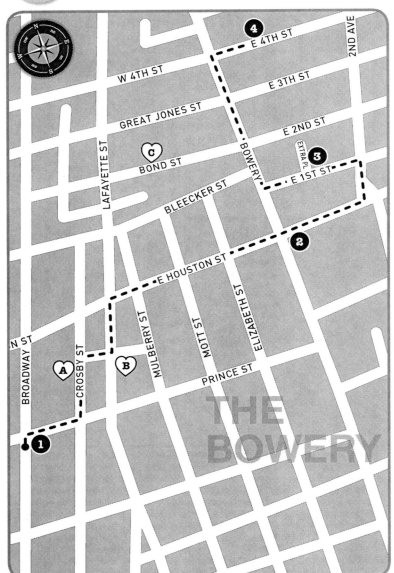

❶ V Chocolates (at Dean & DeLuca):

560 Broadway (@ Prince Street)

We showcased Ron Best and his company, V Chocolates, but Dean & Deluca is a foodie's paradise with gorgeous food and chocolates.

❷ Azure Chocolat (at Whole Foods Market):

95 E Houston Street (@ Bowery)

When passing through the store from Bowery to Chrystie, we find it nearly impossible to avoid stopping at the deluxe chocolate counter for Azure truffles. The butterfly logo symbolizes the transformation one experiences when eating an amazing piece of chocolate.

❸ Bespoke Chocolates:

6 Extra Place (@ E 1st Street)

Nestled on an unassuming dead-end alley, this little shop has been recognized nationally. Rachel Zoe Insler is in tune with the palates of many.

❹ Bond Street Chocolates:

63 E 4th Street (between Bowery and 2nd Avenue)

Edgy, yet elegant, there are some wicked and boozy concoctions that are handmade in the kitchen behind the counter. Visit soon and hope that the Cachaça Bonbon is available.

Is chocolate as good as sex? Chocolate contains phenylethylalanine, which is an opiate produced by our brains when we are falling in love. It is also very adequately produced during sex, providing intense feelings of ecstasy.

The Bowery LOCAL STOPS

Ⓐ Housing Works Bookstore and Café:

126 Crosby Street (between Houston and Prince Streets)

Eat, drink, read, and be merry all while supporting a great cause.

Ⓑ Lafco New York:

285 Lafayette Street (between Jersey and Prince Streets)

This store oozes luxury. It was featured on Oprah. Check in for the latest availability of imported chocolates.

Ⓒ The Smile:

26 Bond Street (between Lafayette Street and Bowery)

Infinitely charming and somewhat hidden eatery that we frequent. Try the chocolate and brie baguette. We insist on it!

The Bowery XOCOATL FOOTPATH

1 V Chocolates
(at Dean and DeLuca)

560 Broadway
New York, NY 10012
212.226.6800 (Dean and DeLuca)
801.269.8444 (V Chocolates)
vchocolates.com

CHOCOLATIER:
Ron Best

CHOCOLATE USED:
· Barry Callebaut

History:

In the experience section below we have noted the three or so chocolatiers that are usually on display at Dean & Deluca. However, the high quality chocolates of Roni-Sue, Christopher Norman and Fritz Knipschildt are highlighted in other chapters of this book, thus making space for the Utah-based shop of V Chocolates.

Ron Best started making chocolates over 20 years ago, and by all means is a very talented chocolatier. Not too long ago, Best had to give up the chocolate business and actually started selling insurance for a few years. His gift of crafting chocolate wouldn't let him stay out of the kitchen though, and in 2004, V Chocolates was resurrected.

So popular, and tasty, has V Chocolates become, that it has been the recipient of the "Best in State" award in 2008 and 2009 for Utah's

best candies and confections. More V Chocolates outlets can be found out west, but for now, Dean & Deluca, and Barney's (660 Madison Ave) remain the only two in New York City. Ron Best and company specialize in fresh ingredients, including Belgian chocolate, and gorgeous packaging, making V Chocolates ideal for gifting.

If you're looking for another reason to try V Chocolates, know that they are fully Kosher-certified by OU Kosher. Best and company have gone out of their way to meet these requirements, along with making chocolate that remains fresh and delectable after its cross-country trip.

Experience:

For us, chocolate falls under the large umbrella of enjoying not only yummy hand-crafted delights, but food in general. If you're anything like us, the foodie paradise of Dean &

HOURS:
Mon—Fri: 7am—8am
Sat and Sun: 8am—8pm

SUBWAYS:
N, R to Prince Street
B, D, F, M to Broadway/Lafayette
Street

SHIPPING:
Online ordering and shipping from
Utah. Corporate gifts and fundraising
opportunities available.

ADDITIONAL INFO:
Kosher-certified

DeLuca will surely leave you swooning. Shiny fruit, vegetables sprinkled with just the right amount of water, high-end coffee, and, of course, a well-manicured chocolate display case.

In the middle of this high-end grocery store lies a cornucopia of chocolate treasures mainly from New York chocolatiers. Christopher Norman's, Fritz Knipschildt and Roni-Sue's chocolate each receive their due, but surprisingly enough, V Chocolates is also quite conspicuous. At stores like Dean and Deluca, its a bit of a guess what will be on display, but our philosophy is to try a couple bonbons or truffles from each of the various chocolatiers. Excessive? Not if you plan on walking it off.

Dean & DeLuca, though sometimes crowded, can be an edifying experience. There are not many places that have a selection of chocolates from around the city, or the country for that matter, so be fearless and go head-to-head. Comparing different confections from around the city all in one location is a great way to be introduced to the seductive world of eating fine chocolate. We highly recommend it.

The Bowery XOCOATL FOOTPATH

V Chocolates
Purchases

Truffles & Bonbons:

Name/Description:

_____ Rating: ☆☆☆☆☆

Name/Description:

_____ Rating: ☆☆☆☆☆

Name/Description:

_____ Rating: ☆☆☆☆☆

Name/Description:

_____ Rating: ☆☆☆☆☆

Bars & Barks:

Name/Description:

_____ Rating: ☆☆☆☆☆

Name/Description:

_____ Rating: ☆☆☆☆☆

Name/Description:

_____ Rating: ☆☆☆☆☆

Drinks & Others:

Name/Description:

_____ Rating: ☆☆☆☆☆

Name/Description:

_____ Rating: ☆☆☆☆☆

Notes:

_____

_____

_____

_____

_____

_____

_____

_____

_____

_____

_____

_____

Share your feedback with us @ professorchocolate.com

The Bowery **XOCOATL FOOTPATH**

2 Azure Chocolat
(at Whole Foods Market)
95 E Houston Street
New York, NY 10002
212.420.1320 (Whole Foods)
631.425.1885 (Azure Chocolat)
azurechocolat.com

CHOCOLATIER:
Heather Foley

CHOCOLATE USED:
· Barry Callebaut

History:

The repeating phrase on the Azure website is, "All you need is love and chocolate..." We couldn't agree more! Azure Chocolat opened its doors in the spring of 2004 in Centerport, NY. Heather Foley, founder, is yet another successful woman from the corporate world who has turned to chocolate making in a move toward creative expression and self-fulfillment. Wanting to see her children grow and to spend more time with them drove Foley to start the company. A passion for infusing different cultural influences into her recipes has allowed her creativity and her penchant for the expression of love to blossom.

Ties with the corporate world haven't been cut completely though. Azure offers an impressive array of custom corporate gifts with the personal touches of handwritten notes and the ability to attach one's own company logo to the gift as well. She seems to have achieved

a savory/sweet balance in her business model as well as in her individual chocolate pieces. Foley loves making people happy with her chocolate. This idea is one of the main inspirations for this book! She describes the wave of euphoria that washes over some of her customers as they taste her delightfully engineered concoctions. Care for customer needs is also evident in the fact that the entire production facility is Kosher certified and dedicated gluten-free. Foley gives away a free box of chocolate each month based on customer stories submitted through her website.

The stories are meant to nominate someone who, for one reason of another, deserves a no-strings-attached box of chocolate delivered to their doorstep. This reminds us of the movie Bed of Roses in which the owner of a flower shop delivers all of the floral orders personally just to see the expression on the recipients' faces.

The Bowery XOCOATL FOOTPATH

HOURS:
Mon—Sun: 8am—11am

SUBWAYS:
F to 2nd Avenue
B, D to Broadway/Lafayette Sreet

SHIPPING:
There is an online order form which
can be faxed, emailed, or dropped off
to Azure Chocolat, located in Centerport, NY.

ADDITIONAL INFO:
Gluten-free and Kosher-certified

Experience:

Azure is the perfect compliment to round out the atmosphere in the Whole Foods Market in the Bowery. While the store is a mecca for both lo-cally produced and imported gustatorial fare, it can be somewhat overwhelming because of its sheer size. The fact that they bring an entire army of purveyors under one roof leads us to visit and shop frequently. One of the values of Whole Foods is to "satisfy and delight their cus-tomers." As far as we are concerned, the addition of vendors like Azure Chocolat completely accomplishes this.

Currently, there are dozens of Gluten-free, Kosher-certified truffles available both on the website and at this Whole Foods. They adorn the showcase in the chocolate section at the Bowery and Houston location. Her masterpieces stand their ground amongst the mixed selection of truffles while maintaining an air of simple, elegant charm. The truffles are hand-rolled and are made in small batches along with a with a delectable selection of barks, toffees, and brown-ies which are collectively referred to as "Chocolat Comforts."

We recommend visiting the Centerport store also, as a celebra-tion of chocolate. While you're there, try raising the Dubbel Dark Ale Truffle and make a toast to Azure Chocolat, to Heather Foley, and to Whole Foods for bringing her creations to the big city.

The Bowery XOCOATL FOOTPATH

Azure Chocolat Purchases

Truffles & Bonbons:

Name/Description:

Rating: ☆☆☆☆☆

Name/Description:

Rating: ☆☆☆☆☆

Name/Description:

Rating: ☆☆☆☆☆

Name/Description:

Rating: ☆☆☆☆☆

Bars & Barks:

Name/Description:

Rating: ☆☆☆☆☆

Name/Description:

Rating: ☆☆☆☆☆

Name/Description:

Rating: ☆☆☆☆☆

Drinks & Others:

Name/Description:

Rating: ☆☆☆☆☆

Name/Description:

Rating: ☆☆☆☆☆

XOCOATL FOOTPATH

Notes:

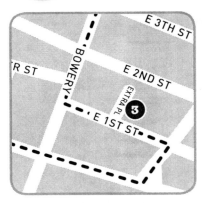

❸ Bespoke Chocolates

6 Extra Place
New York, NY 10003
212.260.7103
bespokechocolates.com

CHOCOLATIER:
Rachel Zoe Insler

CHOCOLATE USED:
· Valrhona
· Santander
· El Rey
· Michel Cluizel

History:

Former neuroscientist-turned-chocolatier Rachel Zoe Insler, started Bespoke Chocolates in 2008. Bespoke, which means custom-made, is a perfect descriptor for the types of truffles she crafts. The affable and smiley Insler first got the idea of opening a chocolate shop while attending grad school at Columbia University, where she was aiming for a cognitive neuroscience degree. Fortunately for us, Insler missed the personal interaction and creativity that one is sometimes not afforded while attending graduate school. Bespoke combines the essence of human interaction and creativity into one petite boutique.

Insler derives much inspiration from her overseas training and traveling, when she samples chocolates the world over. Her specialized training is from none other than the master chocolatier, Keith Hurdman, at London's Melt Chocolates.

With her training and talent, Insler has been able to negotiate the complex world of buying beans and creating what we so deeply crave: hand-crafted chocolate. In an interview with Adam Roberts, of the Amateur Gourmet, Insler explains why her chocolates are so unique: "Most chocolate shops have all the same kind of chocolate and only differentiate between levels of darkness as opposed to where the beans come from. Here, we choose different chocolates from different parts of the world to match the different fillings." This is nothing short of a master's pin-pointed perfection and attention to detail.

Experience:

Triumph! That's how we felt when we found the bite-size shop, Bespoke. Do not be deterred by the lack of signage, but do look for the chalkboard sign at the corner of Extra Place and 1st Street. Not even half-way down the pint-sized alley is the fairly young outfit of Rachel Zoe

The Bowery XOCOATL FOOTPATH

HOURS:
Tue—Fri: 11am—7pm
Sat and Sun: 12pm—8pm
Closed Mondays

SUBWAYS:
F to 2nd Avenue
B, D to Broadway/Lafayette Street
6 to Bleecker Street

SHIPPING:
Boxes of chocolate can be shipped via
FedEx 2-day delivery. Orders sent out
every Tuesday. Courier service
available for local delivery.

ADDITIONAL INFO:
Vegetarian and vegan options available

Insler's, Bespoke. Bespoke's sanctuary of labor-intensive confections awaits your hunger for delicately made bonbons.

The shop itself is on the ground floor of a modern apartment building with gleaming steel and wide windows. As cool as the exterior is, the bite-size interior of Bespoke is tranquil and warm. Once you've stepped inside, observe the handsomely displayed confections on the left, always made fresh daily. Tiptoe your way to the unobstructed view of the kitchen and become captivated by the talented Insler hard at work. All of her handcrafted morsels are composed on-site in the compact kitchen.

Though the selection is small, her confections are amongst the more unique and creative including the award-winning Pretzel-Covered Sea-Salted Caramels. Your taste buds will be swooned by a mélange of flavors, possibly forcing you to break out in ecstatic dance, we certainly did. One of our favorite non-truffle items is the Bespoke version of Nutella. The smooth infusion of chocolate and hazelnut had us simultaneously driveling. Good on bread and by the spoonful, or both!

Bespoke, though without seating, is warm and inviting, always compelling us to linger long after we have voraciously consumed our treats. You can do the same. For something new on the palate, try the Southampton Tea Truffle: a combination of an apricot-induced black Ceylon tea with Caribbean chocolate.

The Bowery PROFESSOR PICKS

May we suggest our favorites?
• Pretzel-Covered Sea-Salted Caramels
• Homemade Hazelnut Spread

Bespoke Chocolates Purchases

Truffles & Bonbons:

Name/Description:

Rating: ☆☆☆☆☆

Name/Description:

Rating: ☆☆☆☆☆

Name/Description:

Rating: ☆☆☆☆☆

Name/Description:

Rating: ☆☆☆☆☆

Bars & Barks:

Name/Description:

Rating: ☆☆☆☆☆

Name/Description:

Rating: ☆☆☆☆☆

Name/Description:

Rating: ☆☆☆☆☆

Drinks & Others:

Name/Description:

Rating: ☆☆☆☆☆

Name/Description:

Rating: ☆☆☆☆☆

Notes:

The Bowery **XOCOATL FOOTPATH**

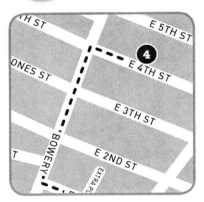

④ Bond Street Chocolate

63 E 4th Street
New York, NY 10003
212.677.5103
bondstchocolate.com

CHOCOLATIER:
Lynda Stern

CHOCOLATE USED:
· Valrhona
· E. Guittard

History:

Bond Street Chocolate was created a few years ago by Lynda Stern and her husband Scott. In its current location on 4th Street, Scott was responsible for the interior design of the shop, which is extraordinarily exquisite, while Lynda has been, and remains, responsible for the chocolate and the infusion of the tipple ingredients.

For a former pastry chef, the experience of owning and running her own boutique has always been an organic one. She began making chocolate-covered figures of iconic people like Jesus and Moses many years ago. Lucky for us, this turned into the business that we know and love today.

We should set the record straight and mention that while, yes, this is Bond Street Chocolate, it is not on Bond Street. It is on 4th Street. Bond Street Chocolate, though not as hid-

den as Bespoke, has a mysteriously posh quality to it.

Experience:

A few steps down leads into the cozy lair of Bond Street Chocolates. Exposed brick on one side and a sultry black, velvety wall paper on the other offers any visitor a sumptuous chocolate-tasting ambiance. Mind you we haven't even touched on the chocolate yet.

On a daily basis, 10-12 sumptuous truffles and bonbons are displayed, freshly made in the back behind the counter. Stern is constantly changing the interior infusions and always searching for new and intriguing ingredients.

We are certainly intrigued by the intoxicated bonbons like Absinthe, Elderflower Liqueur, and, if you're lucky, Cachaça. Most unique is that the piquant, creamy interior of these bon-

The Bowery XOCOATL FOOTPATH

HOURS:
Tues—Sat: 12am—8pm
Sun: 1pm—5pm
Closed Monday

SUBWAYS:
N, R to Prince Street
B, D to Broadway/ Lafayette Street
F to 2nd Avenue

SHIPPING:
Shipping available when ordering by
phone

ADDITIONAL INFO:
Vegetarian and vegan options available

bons touch on something that New York City chocolatiers are so adept at crafting: unique and nonpareil flavors that can't be found in a department store box. It is infusions like these that inspire some to write a whole book...

Bond Street Chocolate is not limited to small-batched bonbons. Chocolate skulls that have an edgy "rock'n'roll" feel are also available, and are delicious despite looking like pieces of jewelry. Stern also creates gold-leafed chocolate statues of Jesus, Moses, the Virgin Guadalupe, and Ganesh, all of course edible and very delectable.

Time permitting, sit at the tiny table for two and listen to the cacoph-

ony of locals coming and going and chatting it up with Stern. Of course this is all the more fun when you savor, and not devour, the chocolate before you.

The Bowery PROFESSOR PICKS
May we suggest our favorites?
• Milk Chocolate Bar with Caramelized Almonds and Sea Salt
• Elderflower Liqueur Bonbons

The Bowery XOCOATL FOOTPATH

Bond Street Chocolate Purchases

Truffles & Bonbons:

Name/Description:

Rating: ☆☆☆☆☆

Name/Description:

Rating: ☆☆☆☆☆

Name/Description:

Rating: ☆☆☆☆☆

Name/Description:

Rating: ☆☆☆☆☆

Bars & Barks:

Name/Description:

Rating: ☆☆☆☆☆

Name/Description:

Rating: ☆☆☆☆☆

Name/Description:

Rating: ☆☆☆☆☆

Drinks & Others:

Name/Description:

Rating: ☆☆☆☆☆

Name/Description:

Rating: ☆☆☆☆☆

73

Notes:

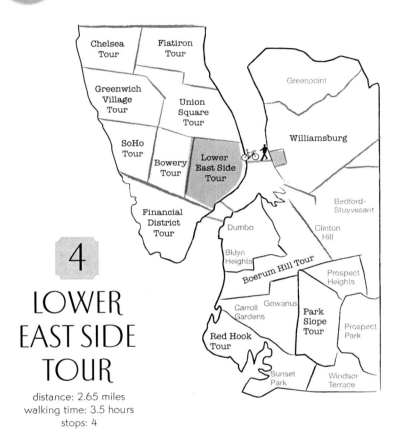

Chelsea
Tour

Flatiron
Tour

Greenpoint

Greenwich
Village
Tour

Union
Square
Tour

Williamsburg

SoHo
Tour

Bowery
Tour

Lower
East Side
Tour

Financial
District
Tour

Bedford-
Stuyvesant

Dumbo

Clinton
Hill

Bklyn
Heights

Boerum Hill Tour

Prospect
Heights

Carroll
Gardens

Gowanus

Park
Slope
Tour

Prospect
Park

Red Hook
Tour

Sunset
Park

Windsor
Terrace

4

LOWER EAST SIDE TOUR

distance: 2.65 miles
walking time: 3.5 hours
stops: 4

Undergoing rapid gentrification for the last 10 years or so is the historic Lower East Side neighborhood, located in the southeastern pocket of Manhattan. Rough borders include Houston and Canal Streets to the north and south along with Allen and Essex Streets to the west and east. For much of its history, the LES has been home to many immigrant populations, even being called "Little Germany" or "Kleindeutschland" at one point. Historic synagogues are found amidst trendy restaurants and shops, while old buildings remain in the shadow of shiny new constructions. The LES is as authentic as NYC gets, a collision of old and new; traditional and trendy.

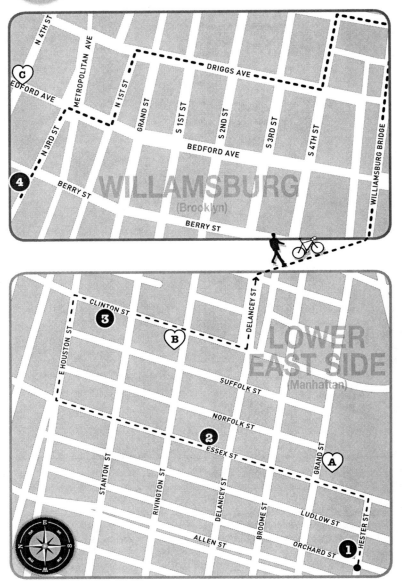

Lower East Side BRIDGE TOUR

1 The Sweet Life:
63 Hester Street (@ Ludlow Street)
Selling everything from chocolate to obscure European treats, this venerable candy shop has been around for quite some time. Their online catalog is expansive, not to mention that they deliver the world over.

2 Roni-Sue's Chocolate Shoppe (at Essex Street Market):
120 Essex Street (between Delancey and Rivington Streets)
Nestled within the hustle and bustle of the Essex Street Market, Rhonda Kave, a.k.a. Roni-Sue, blends her crisp 'n' porky concoctions of chocolate and bacon. Try the Pig Candy for something new and adventurous.

3 Cocoa Bar:
21 Clinton Street (between Houston and Stanton Streets)
Is it a chocolate boutique? Is it a cafe? Is it a dessert destination with wine pairings? Luckily it's all of the above. Enter here for your tranquil dose of chocolate and wine. Could there be a better combination?

4 Mast Brothers Chocolate:
105a N 3rd Street (between Berry and Wythe Streets)
In one of the few "bean to bar" enterprises in the U.S., the brothers Mast can be found creating chocolate from the 50lb burlap sacks of cacao beans.

Lower East Side LOCAL STOPS

> Cocoa butter is the pure fat that exists in cacao beans. It is solid at room temperature and melts at about 97° F. This conveniently allows chocolate to literally melt in your mouth.

A Doughnut Plant:
379 Grand Street (@ Norfolk Street)
Where do all of the incredibly fresh and intoxicating doughnuts at the high-end gourmet food stores come from? They come from the Doughnut Plant. Try the Valrhona Chocolate flavor.

B San Marzano's Brick Oven Pizza:
71 Clinton Street (@ Rivington Street)
We never expected to simultaneously discover our favorite pizza and brunch on that fateful day... but we did. To top it off, the owners were incredibly friendly and cheerful.

C Bedford Cheese Shop:
229 Bedford Avenue (@ N 4th Street)
A small staff of knowledgeable cheesemongers in an old-fashioned shop providing the finest quality cheeses from around the world.

❶ The Sweet Life

63 Hester Street
New York, NY 10002
212.598.0092
sweetlifeny.com

OWNERS:
Sam Greenfield
Diane Miller

CHOCOLATE USED:
· Barry Callebaut

History:

The Sweet Life opened in the heart of the Lower East Side in 1982. Since then, it has been rated among the top candy and chocolate shops in NYC. It would seem unusual to describe a store as both adorable and chic, but The Sweet Life fits both bills. Their trays of chocolate-covered treats and dried fruits have received acclaim from critics and foodies everywhere. The store's motto is "anything can be dipped in chocolate." With their own chocolate machines, the owners offer exclusive and fresh handmade products daily.

This old-school candy shop has developed an impressive resume with virtually no marketing. The website is organized by category and also by color; this allows anyone wishing to create a custom gift to do so by organizing confections according to a chosen color scheme. The stylists

from Martha Stewart Living have turned to the store for inspiration and the creative director for Kate Spade was once quoted as saying that her favorite accessory is a bag of pistachios from this Hester Street landmark.

Ownership has changed since the store opened more than 25 years ago, but the quality and ambiance has not. Brother-sister team Sam Greenfield and Diane Miller bought the tiny neighborhood shop in 2004. They stocked the shelves from floor to ceiling with the finest selection of sweet treats from around the world. It is one of the few places in the city where real old-fashioned fudge and bulk Barry Callebaut chocolate can be found virtually side by side.

Lower East Side BRIDGE TOUR

HOURS:
Mon—Fri: 10am—6:30pm
Sat and Sun: 11am—6pm

SUBWAYS:
F to East Broadway
B, D to Grand Street

SHIPPING:
All orders shipped within five business days anywhere in the U.S.
International shipping upon request.

Experience:

The experience of visiting The Sweet Life is really defined by the store's name. The first time we visited, we couldn't help but feel as though we had been there before. It is what a high-end "sweets" store should be in our opinion. If you could imagine walking into Willy Wonka's private study, it would probably pale in comparison to this small shop. It is truly the grown-up, sophisticated version of the traditional economy candy store and the classic mom-and-pop-shop rolled into one.

With offerings of varietal honey, hard-to-find quality candy, and imported chocolate, you may leave with much more than you bargained for. The moment you walk through the door the scintillating aroma alone will invigorate the dullest of senses. Feast on the esoteric selection of sweets and snacks, and appreciate the store's name to a degree of recognition that it truly deserves.

Lower East Side PROFESSOR PICKS

May we suggest our favorites?
• PB&J Graham Cracker Sandwich (dipped in chocolate)
• Dark Chocolate-Covered Ginger Slices

The Sweet Life
Purchases

Truffles & Bonbons:

Name/Description:

Rating: ☆☆☆☆☆

Name/Description:

Rating: ☆☆☆☆☆

Name/Description:

Rating: ☆☆☆☆☆

Name/Description:

Rating: ☆☆☆☆☆

Bars & Barks:

Name/Description:

Rating: ☆☆☆☆☆

Name/Description:

Rating: ☆☆☆☆☆

Name/Description:

Rating: ☆☆☆☆☆

Drinks & Others:

Name/Description:

Rating: ☆☆☆☆☆

Name/Description:

Rating: ☆☆☆☆☆

Notes:

Share your feedback with us @ professorchocolate.com

❷ Roni-Sue's Chocolate Shoppe
(at Essex Street Market)
120 Essex Street
New York, NY 10002
212.260.0241
roni-sue.com

OWNERS:
Rhonda Kave (a.k.a. Roni-Sue)

CHOCOLATE USED:
· Barry Callebaut

History:

Roni-Sue's chocolate has rocketed itself into foodies lore by making some of the most original chocolate-covered-fatty masterpieces out there. Located in the food paradise of the Essex Street Market, Roni-Sue's has created quite a niche. This is not the niche of over-zealous packaging or prepossessing chocolate-covered strawberries. No, this is the niche of chocolate and bacon.

Before the adored Rhonda Kave, a.k.a. Roni-Sue, inflamed the palates of many, yours truly included, she lived on Long Island for 25 years. It wasn't until recently that she and her husband made the move into the city. During those 25 years, Kave made devilishly good butter crunch and truffles from home, especially around the holidays. The part-time hobby was the seed that would one day yield Kave running her own shop.

The idea of owning her own chocolate shop solidified when she was researching farmer's markets and food insecurity for a sociology class at NYU. When Kave visited the Essex Street Market as part of the research project, she became enamored by the market itself along with a small and unused space. It didn't take long for this chocolate mastermind to take the plunge and begin her foray into the choco-porky-making world.

Since opening in 2007, Roni-Sue's has moved to the heavier-trafficked west side of the market, attracting customers the world over.

Experience:

Before you find Roni-Sue's, and please do, you must first locate the Essex Street Market. From the northeast corner of Essex and Delancey, walk a few steps north and you will stumble upon a nondescript entryway into one

HOURS:
Mon—Fri: 11am—7pm
Sat: 10am—7pm

SUBWAYS:
F to Delancey Street
J, M, Z to Essex Street

SHIPPING:
Year-round shipping available via
USPS. Same-day delivery to most
NYC addresses.

h

of the real hidden gems of Manhattan. Besides Roni-Sue's, there are numerous meat and produce shops, a cookie counter, a coffee stand and Saxelby Cheese, another can't miss.

Rhonda Kave, the red-haired and freckle-faced owner of Roni-Sue's, is almost always behind the bonbon-filled display case, smiling and helping eager customers like us who have been clamoring for her edgy collection of bonbons (like Absinthe and Dark and Stormy) inspired by her children's favorite drinks. Though these bonbons are worth your time, it is the Pig Candy that haunts our dreams. Strips of bacon soaked in chocolate create a crunchy-buttery-salty mix. Also part of the col-

lection is the highly-addictive BaCorn. An infusion of popcorn and peanuts sprinkled with caramel, intermixed with the house specialty bacon.

Roni-Sue's chocolates will certainly delight, but so will Rhonda Kave herself. One of the more affable proprietors in New York, she epitomizes the friendly and present store owners of yesteryear. She makes her chocolate and converses with customers with a warm and inviting smile. This is chocolate that is seriously made with love and pride.

Lower East Side PROFESSOR PICKS

May we suggest our favorites?
• Pig Candy
• Strawberry Rhubarb Truffles

Lower East Side **BRIDGE TOUR**

Roni-Sue's Chocolate Shoppe
Purchases

Truffles & Bonbons:

Name/Description:
_____

_____ Rating: ☆☆☆☆☆

Name/Description:
_____

_____ Rating: ☆☆☆☆☆

Name/Description:
_____

_____ Rating: ☆☆☆☆☆

Name/Description:
_____

_____ Rating: ☆☆☆☆☆

Bars & Barks:

Name/Description:
_____

_____ Rating: ☆☆☆☆☆

Name/Description:
_____

_____ Rating: ☆☆☆☆☆

Name/Description:
_____

_____ Rating: ☆☆☆☆☆

Drinks & Others:

Name/Description:
_____

_____ Rating: ☆☆☆☆☆

Name/Description:
_____

_____ Rating: ☆☆☆☆☆

Notes:

We love Roni-Sue!

Share your feedback with us @ professorchocolate.com

❸ Cocoa Bar

21 Clinton Street
New York, NY 10002
212.677.7417
cocoabarnyc.com

STORE OWNERS:
Liat Cohen and Yaniv Reeis

CHOCOLATIER:
Michel Cluizel chocolate is shipped
in from France

History:

Cocoa Bar has two New York City locations, the original is located in Park Slope, Brooklyn, and the second is ensconced in the ever-changing Lower East Side. Owned by the husband-wife team of Liat Cohen and Yaniv Reeis, Cocoa Bar has become a neighborhood fixture in both locations.

The year 2005 marked the beginning for Cocoa Bar, but it didn't come without some major risks for the spouses. One risk was the fact that Park Slope had been, and still is, laden with popular cafés such as Ozzie's, the Tea Lounge, and Starbucks. In the past few years, more cafés have joined the ranks of Park Slope niches, usually enjoying the patronage of the of high-standard-obsessed locals.

Luckily, the trio of bakery/coffee shop/wine house is eclectic and unique, but also popular enough to stay in business. At some point, the Cocoa Bar in both locations may have used Leonidas chocolates, from Belgium. More recently though, we were informed that Michel Cluizel chocolates, sent express from Danville, France, are awaiting your consumption.

Lower East Side BRIDGE TOUR

HOURS:
Sun—Wed: 8am—12am
Thurs—Sat: 8am—2am

SUBWAYS:
F, J, M, Z to Essex Street

Experience:

The Lower East Side location is as laid-back as its Brooklyn counterpart. An intimate seating area and WiFi service make the Cocoa Bar perfect for the studious on a weekday afternoon or the romantic couple looking for an after-dinner dessert snack. The Cocoa Bar can at times feel like an arty coffee shop, but one that sells delicious chocolate and other goodies.

The chocolates are homemade, and are certainly worth sampling, however, you may want to make the most of this visit and indulge in the Cocoa Bar's unique twist when it comes to the sit-down experience.

Though it may be called the Cocoa Bar, it is certainly more than that, and certainly worth your time to order some of the chocolate-infused desserts.

The menu is extensive, and very fun, especially if you like to pair your chocolate with wine. The knowledgeable staff and explanatory menu can make this destination a dining experience unto itself. The scrumptious Flourless Chocolate Cake is a slice of heaven you can enjoy while sipping one of their red wines.

Lower East Side PROFESSOR PICKS

May we suggest our favorites?
- Flourless Chocolate Cake
- The Funky Monkey

Lower East Side BRIDGE TOUR

Cocoa Bar
Purchases

Truffles & Bonbons:

Name/Description:

Rating: ☆☆☆☆☆

Name/Description:

Rating: ☆☆☆☆☆

Name/Description:

Rating: ☆☆☆☆☆

Name/Description:

Rating: ☆☆☆☆☆

Bars & Barks:

Name/Description:

Rating: ☆☆☆☆☆

Name/Description:

Rating: ☆☆☆☆☆

Name/Description:

Rating: ☆☆☆☆☆

Drinks & Others:

Name/Description:

Rating: ☆☆☆☆☆

Name/Description:

Rating: ☆☆☆☆☆

Notes:

④ Mast Brothers Chocolate

105a N 3rd Street
Brooklyn, NY 11211
718.388.2625
mastbrotherschocolate.com

CHOCOLATIERS:
Rick and Michael Mast

CHOCOLATE USED:
The Mast Brothers use beans to produce their own chocolate bars from Madagascar, Venezuela, Dominican Republic, and Ecuador.

History:

The Mast brothers pride themselves on being one of the few "bean to bar" chocolate artisans in the United States, delicately creating small batches of chocolate. Their cacao beans come from all over the world, sent to them in 50- pound burlap sacks. The beans are single-origin Venezuelan and Ecuadorian. Their elegant Italian paper that envelopes the luscious bars stands out in a sea of unremarkable chocolate bar paper and designs.

The two brothers, Rick and Michael, though completely engaged in their enterprise, come to cultivating cacao from different paths. Rick has had experience in a few NYC restaurants such as the SoHo House and the Gramercy Tavern, and he's also spent some time with Jacque Torres. Michael, on the other hand, has spent a considerable amount of time in the finance sector for independent television and film. Both now are completely devoted to the process of making chocolate from choosing beans in Central and South America, to roasting and tempering in their Williamsburg factory.

In a recent interview with brooklynbased.net, Rick Mast stated, "The closer anybody who consumes anything is connected to where it came from, it's going to be a better experience." This is the premise on which the Mast brothers run their tidy business and one more and more people in the food business seem to be following. A closer relationship to the food which we consume produces more responsibility on the part of purveyors and farmers, and food that is simply better for us.

HOURS:
Weekends Only: 12pm—8pm

SUBWAYS:
L to Bedford Avenue

SHIPPING:
Shipping available for U.S. addresses only. Payment online via Paypal.

MAST BROTHERS CHOCOLATE FACTORY

SOURCING CACAO FROM:
PATANEMO, VENEZUELA
OCUMARE, VENEZUELA
SAMBIRANO VALLEY, MADAGASCAR,
DOMINICAN REP. CO OP
CARENERO SUPERIOR, VENEZUELA

Experience:

The bearded brothers Mast only recently opened this tiny and unassuming chocolate shop in Williamsburg, one of the city's more trendy 'hoods. The store itself is minimalist yet hip in décor, but you didn't come here to critique their interior design choices.

The different chocolate bars are displayed in wooden and glass casing, surrounded by a plethora of cacao beans. Descriptions and fun names accompany the bars in the display case, but feel free to ask questions, these guys love what they do and love talking about their trade.

One of their popular bars is the scrumptious yet-not-too-sweet 60% cacao "dark" milk chocolate. Other chocolate bars are infused with pecans, pistachios, almonds, and cranberries. Each bar comes wrapped in Italian paper that could be mistaken for a piece of art.

Mast Brothers Chocolate bars are sold throughout small stores in New York City as well as in a few other states. However, the small trek to the actual "factory" where you can witness the darlings of Williamsburg hard at work, and see 50-pound bags of cacao beans, is worth your while.

Lower East Side PROFESSOR PICKS

May we suggest our favorites?
• Dark Chocolate with Fleur de Sel
• Dark Chocolate with Dried Cranberries

Mast Brothers Chocolate Purchases

Truffles & Bonbons:

Name/Description:

Rating: ☆☆☆☆☆

Name/Description:

Rating: ☆☆☆☆☆

Name/Description:

Rating: ☆☆☆☆☆

Name/Description:

Rating: ☆☆☆☆☆

Bars & Barks:

Name/Description:

Rating: ☆☆☆☆☆

Name/Description:

Rating: ☆☆☆☆☆

Name/Description:

Rating: ☆☆☆☆☆

Drinks & Others:

Name/Description:

Rating: ☆☆☆☆☆

Name/Description:

Rating: ☆☆☆☆☆

Notes:

_____
_____
_____
_____
_____
_____
_____
_____
_____
_____
_____
_____

This is Joanna from BARC, a dog shelter to which proceeds from the sale of this book will be donated.

Share your feedback with us @ professorchocolate.com

94

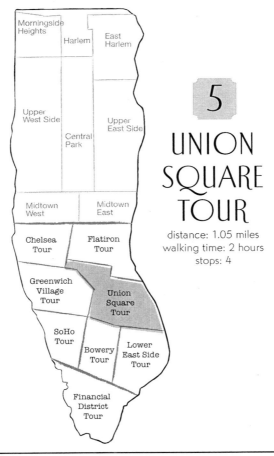

5

UNION SQUARE TOUR

distance: 1.05 miles
walking time: 2 hours
stops: 4

Morningside Heights

Harlem

East Harlem

Upper West Side

Central Park

Upper East Side

Midtown West

Midtown East

Chelsea Tour

Flatiron Tour

Greenwich Village Tour

Union Square Tour

SoHo Tour

Bowery Tour

Lower East Side Tour

Financial District Tour

Situated in the middle of four neighborhoods, Union Square is one of the most central places to meet up in NYC Located between 14th and 17th streets to the north and south, and Broadway and Park Avenue South to the west and east, Union Square is almost always a buzzing beehive. Statues of George Washington and Gandhi are representative of the Square's history of social activism and political demonstrations. On a lighter note, the Square has played host to a plethora of farmers and their fresh goods for the last 30 years. Everything from grass-fed meat to sheep's wool is sold at the outdoor farmer's market four days a week. Be sure to stop by the Patches of Star Goat Dairy stand for some chocolate-covered chevre!

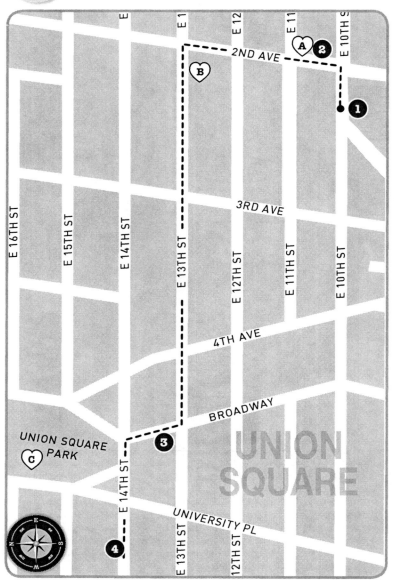

1 Stōgo:

159 2nd Avenue (entrance on 10th Street)
Elevating both our health and palate satisfaction, Stōgo's vegan emphasis is nothing short of delightful..

2 Black Hound :

170 2nd Avenue (@ 11th Street)
On the scene for over two decades in this neighborhood, this elegant boutique creates decadent truffles, cakes, and cookies.

3 Max Brenner:

841 Broadway (between 13th and 14th Streets)
Chic and stylish, the ever-expanding mega-business of Max Brenner offers what few chocolate boutiques in NYC can: a dinner menu. A great touch, but chocolate is still the star.

4 Fritz Knipschildt (at Garden of Eden):

7 East 14th Street (between 5th Avenue and Union Square Park West)
An inexhaustible store with the true gourmand in mind. Let your senses lead you through the chocolate here.

Chocolate has consistently been shown not to cause acne in studies conducted over the last 50 years! Acne is primarily triggered by surging testosterone levels during puberty (in both boys and girls).

Union Square **LOCAL STOPS**

A Liquiteria:

170 2nd Avenue (@ 11th Street)
Cold-pressed fruit and vegetable juices here are fresh and flavorful.

B Momofuku Milk Bar:

207 2nd Avenue (entrance on 13th Street)
Crack pie, compost cookies, burnt honey butter, and soft serve. Everything is addicting here.

C Union Square Greenmarket:

Union Square West (from 15th to 17th Streets @ Park Avenue South)
This world-famous farmer's market hosts over 140 producers each week. Some of our favorites include: Grazin' Angus Acres, Rick's Picks, Roaming Acres Ostrich, and Patches of Star.

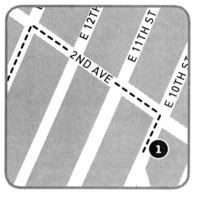

① Stōgo

159 2nd Avenue
(entrance on 10th Street
between 2nd and 3rd Avenues)
New York, NY 10003
212.677.2301
stogonyc.com

OWNERS:
Rob Sedgwick and Steve Horn

History:

A few years ago, as these stories often start, Steve Horn, a successful New York City restauranteur, was having dinner with his friend, Rob Sedgwick, a fledgling actor. Steve presented Rob with the fantastic idea of starting a vegan ice cream store, one where the ice cream was healthy, yet satisfying. Soon enough, the two attended Malcolm Stogo's Ice Cream University.

Malcolm is best known for being the superbrain behind products like Colombo, TCBY, and Häagen Daz. Now try to imagine the two young would-be entrepeneurs presenting the idea of vegan ice cream to the virtual king of ice cream. Stogo at first scoffed at the idea of a soy-based ice cream that uses agave as a natural sweetener.

Eventually, Stogo came on board and was such an inspiration

to the two aspiring store owners, that they decided to use his name for the East Village location. Though ice cream is the main draw at Stogo, their selection of vegan bonbons, truffles, and bars verges on blissful.

Experience:

Stogo's listed address is 159 2nd Avenue, however, the entrance is actually located on the south side of 10th street, across from an old church.

Union Square REFINED & RAW

CHOCOLATE AVAILABLE:

BARS
- Fine and Raw
- NibMor
- Gnosis
- Raw Chocolate Love

TRUFFLES
- Missionary Chocolates
- French Broad
- Fine and Raw
- Cocoa V

HOURS:
Sun—Thurs: 11am—11pm
Fri and Sat: 11am—12Midnight

SUBWAYS:
6 to Astor Place
L to 3rd Avenue

The vegan ice cream draws the customers, and it is certainly stellar, but there are fresh vegan truffles and bonbons for your enjoyment. Vegan? Yes. Vapid and tasteless? No. The chocolate and ice cream is all-natural, without preservatives, and good for you. The homemade ice creams are all made from soy, coconut, or hemp bases, and they use agave instead of refined sugar. The pomegranate with chocolate chips is flavorful and creamy and leaves not one iota of stomach growls, just pure happiness.

"Where's the chocolate?" Stogo sources their vegan chocolate bars from the very best vegan chocolate makers the United States has to of-fer: Fine and Raw, Nibmor, Gnosis, and Raw Chocolate Love. The excellent truffles are from Missionary Chocolates in Oregon, French Broad in North Carolina, and the New York City outfits of Fine and Raw and Cocoa V. All of it is delicious, and perhaps more importantly, it's some of the healthiest around.

There are not many chocolate shops dedicated to vegan treats, so when we find tasty alternatives, we feel it is important to pledge our continued support. Besides, the Vanilla Salted-Caramel Bonbons are delicious enough to keep us satisfied for a week.

Stōgo
Purchases

Truffles & Bonbons:

Name/Description:

Rating: ☆☆☆☆☆

Name/Description:

Rating: ☆☆☆☆☆

Name/Description:

Rating: ☆☆☆☆☆

Name/Description:

Rating: ☆☆☆☆☆

Bars & Barks:

Name/Description:

Rating: ☆☆☆☆☆

Name/Description:

Rating: ☆☆☆☆☆

Name/Description:

Rating: ☆☆☆☆☆

Drinks & Others:

Name/Description:

Rating: ☆☆☆☆☆

Name/Description:

Rating: ☆☆☆☆☆

Notes:

_____

_____

_____

_____

_____

_____

_____

_____

_____

_____

_____

Share your feedback with us @ professorchocolate.com

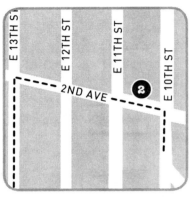
❷ Black Hound

170 2nd Avenue
New York, NY 10003
800.344.4417
212.979.9505
blackhoundny.com

CHOCOLATE USED:
Belgian

History:

Started in the late '80s, Black Hound has been a East Village institution for quite some time and has received numerous awards for its velvety chocolate truffles. All products are made onsite, using Belgian chocolate and the purest of ingredients, with a dedicated eye toward perfection.

Many reviewers of Black Hound rave about their transcendent goods, but not much exists on the actual history of the place. To provide the most comprehensive detail, we'd like to share a quote directly from their website:

"With an impeccable combination of old world, European-inspired baking coupled with artfully simple aesthetics, Black Hound New York has been enchanting palates since 1988. Through rich flavor combinations, superior craftsmanship and natural, always fresh ingredients, Black Hound New York creates an extraordinary array of delights made entirely from scratch and individually created to fulfill each order." We

couldn't say it better ourselves.

Experience:

Though there is not a large variety of truffles to choose from at this venerable shop, chocolate is the main ingredient for many of their splendid confections. Cakes and cookies line the shelves, while the actual truffles are in a display case toward the back of the store. The truffles come in all shapes and sizes and are quite different from the bonbons that you have noticed at other venues. Nonetheless, there's de-

Union Square REFINED & RAW

HOURS:
Mon—Thurs: 10am—10:30pm
Fri and Sat: 10am—11:30pm
Sun: 11am—10pm

SUBWAYS:
L to 1st Avenue or 3rd Avenue
6 to Astor Place

SHIPPING:
Orders placed by noon will be shipped out the same day via UPS.

ADDITIONAL INFO:
Flourless, nut-free, and sugar-free products available

signer-crafted chocolate waiting to be devoured.

Black Hound specializes in showcasing elegance and refinement, so everything here is supposed to taste as good as it looks, which, in our humble opinion, certainly is true. The Busy Bee personal cake is their signature dessert. Find out for yourself why it remains one of the more popular items. The heart-melting chocolate-covered strawberries and rich, buttery cookies are great for bringing to a party or otherwise giving as gifts.

Unfortunately (or maybe fortunately), the Black Hound designers left no room for tables and chairs—the space is chock full of heavenly orbs of

chocolate and personalized cakes, all made in small batches.

If you're aching for a place to sit and savor your treats, try the church yard across the street. Or if you walk about five blocks north you will run into an even more peaceful spot at Stuyvesant Square, a favorite of ours.

Black Hound Purchases

Truffles & Bonbons:

Name/Description: _____

_____ Rating: ☆☆☆☆☆

Name/Description: _____

_____ Rating: ☆☆☆☆☆

Name/Description: _____

_____ Rating: ☆☆☆☆☆

Name/Description: _____

_____ Rating: ☆☆☆☆☆

Bars & Barks:

Name/Description: _____

_____ Rating: ☆☆☆☆☆

Name/Description: _____

_____ Rating: ☆☆☆☆☆

Name/Description: _____

_____ Rating: ☆☆☆☆☆

Drinks & Others:

Name/Description: _____

_____ Rating: ☆☆☆☆☆

Name/Description: _____

_____ Rating: ☆☆☆☆☆

Union Square REFINED & RAW

Notes:

Share your feedback with us @ professorchocolate.com

Union Square REFINED & RAW

❸ Max Brenner

841 Broadway
New York, NY 10003
212.388.0030
maxbrenner.com

CHOCOLATIER:
Oded Brenner

History:

Who is Max Brenner? There are conceivably many Max Brenners on Earth, but not one of them is the founder or principal chocolatier of this mega-company. The name Max Brenner is actually a combination of Max Fichtman and Oded Brenner, two chocolatiers who launched the business in Israel, circa 1995. Dates vary, but the business was sold by 2001 to Strauss-Elite, an Israeli food conglomerate, (think of the Israeli version of General Mills). Not too long after the sale, Max Fichtman bowed out of the enterprise. Oded Brenner, the "bald man," is still in the picture, literally, and has taken on the persona of Max Brenner, while remaining a fixture in the world's chocolate scene.

These days, Max Brenner is opening up stores the world over, from Philadelphia to a planned Boston location and all the way to the Philippines, Sin-

gapore, and, of course, Israel. "Global growth" and a "chocolate culture concept" seems to be what the company emphasizes. With all of that being said, Max Brenner is not just about truffles, pralines, and bonbons, it has become a dessert destination unto its own with a selection of many fine dishes.

Experience:

Make no mistake, the Max Brenner experience is similar to walking into a Hard Rock Cafe, but instead of framed guitars of rock gods, there is a panoply of chocolate accoutrements and products. Max Brenner provides a triple dose of chocolate in the form of the store, the take-out section, and the full-service restaurant with, of course, chocolate as the star.

On a few occasions we have been lucky enough to meet Oded Brenner while he was in town checking out the Union Square location. He happens to

HOURS:
Mon—Thurs: 9am—Midnight
Fri: 9am—2am
Sat: 9am—2am (brunch: 9am—4pm)
Sun: 9am—11pm (brunch: 9am—4pm)

Reservations can be made online or
by phone for visits between 9am and
2pm Monday through Friday.

SHIPPING:
Online and phone orders accepted and
shipped via FedEx next day if received
by 6pm. Courier service in Manhattan is
available for same-day delivery.

SUBWAYS:
L, N, Q, R, 4, 5, 6 to Union
Square/14th Street

be full of smiles and positive energy,
something that reverberates through
the staff. Large in scale, this is a destination for chocoholics who enjoy the
overdose of a chocolate-themed menu.
We recommend the gift of the chocolate syringe, a present for your cocoa-
craving friend who couldn't make the
trip.

As far as chocolate places in New
York City, there really is nothing quite
like the Max Brenner experience in re-
gards to the expansive menu and product line. It is a feast for the senses that
captures everyone who enters into this
chocolate kingdom.

Union Square PROFESSOR PICKS
May we suggest our favorites?
• Suckao (dark)
• Peanut Butter Chunky Chocolate Crepes

Max Brenner
Purchases

Truffles & Bonbons:

Name/Description:

Rating: ☆☆☆☆☆

Name/Description:

Rating: ☆☆☆☆☆

Name/Description:

Rating: ☆☆☆☆☆

Name/Description:

Rating: ☆☆☆☆☆

Bars & Barks:

Name/Description:

Rating: ☆☆☆☆☆

Name/Description:

Rating: ☆☆☆☆☆

Name/Description:

Rating: ☆☆☆☆☆

Drinks & Others:

Name/Description:

Rating: ☆☆☆☆☆

Name/Description:

Rating: ☆☆☆☆☆

Union Square REFINED & RAW

Notes:

Share your feedback with us @ professorchocolate.com

Union Square **REFINED & RAW**

**❹ Fritz Knipschildt
(at Garden of Eden)**
7 East 14th Street
New York, NY 10003
212.255.4200
knipschildt.com

CHOCOLATIER:
Fritz Knipschildt

CHOCOLATE USED:
· Valrhona
· Michel Cluizel
· Belcolade

History:

The Danish-born and educated Fritz Knipschildt arrived in America 15 years ago and, since then, has been treating us with some of the most celebrated and awarded chocolate. Since his teenage years, Knipschildt has been working with very passionate chefs, who have inspired him to make "classic chocolate with a modern twist."

Formally trained in Denmark as a pastry chef in the early '90s, Knipschildt brought his ambition and considerable talent to the U.S., in 1996, when he made chocolates out of his one bedroom apartment. Three years later, Knipschildt officially opened up business on Main Street in Norwalk, CT where he currently creates his masterpieces out of a 6,000-square-foot chocolate and pastry kitchen. Chocopologie Café opened in 2005 as an extension of the already existing, and booming, chocolate kitchen. Here, visitors and customers alike can

immerse themselves in the world of chocolate. Onlookers have the opportunity to gaze through large windows that allows one to "peek in" on the daily operations of the chocolate and pastry factory.

Can't make the trip to Norwalk? No problem. Knipschildt supplies about 900 vendors worldwide, including a handful of the boutiques profiled in this book. Whole Foods Market, Dean & DeLuca, the Chocolate Room, and Garden of Eden are a few in New York City.

Numerous accolades have been bestowed upon Knipschildt , including Gourmet magazine listing him as one of the "top 3 chocolatiers in the world."

Experience:

Garden of Eden store owner and company founder, Mustafa Coskun, brings to life the store's marketing slogan, "A temptation in every aisle." Being in the store is like

Union Square REFINED & RAW

HOURS:
Mon—Sat: 7am—10pm
Sun: 7am—9:30pm

SUBWAYS:
L, N, Q, R, 4, 5, 6 to Union
Square/14th Street
F, M to 14th Street
L to 6th Avenue

SHIPPING INFO:
Same-day (within Manhattan) and
next-day shipping.

ADDITIONAL INFO:
Shop at Knipschildt.com for a full
description of all of the truffles and
treats offered.

"Me, a Chocolatier"
make-your-own bonbons!

walking into one of the cornucopia that one colored diligently in grade school during the Thanksgiving season. To add to this image, imagine looking up and seeing dozens and dozens of picnic-style baskets hanging from the ceiling.

The Garden of Eden is one of several gourmet shops that offers the customer the ability to stock a basket with as many exotic and flavorful treats as possible and then to ship the entire package out to anyone they choose, anywhere in the country.

The display case where the chocolate is housed just seems to fit into its surroundings at this culinary mecca. Even though there are over

ten thousand specialty food items in the store, Fritz's truffles rank among the top 10 for us. One truffle in particular, the Hannah, holds a very special place in our hearts. It has been a running joke of ours that a person must not stare directly at anyone the first time they eat one, because they could quite possibly spontaneously fall in love. It will be hard enough not to fall in love with whichever one of Knipschildt's "ladies" you decide to indulge in. Any of these Belgian-style jewels will have you coming back for more again and again (and again).

Union Square REFINED & RAW

Fritz Knipschildt
Purchases

Truffles & Bonbons:

Name/Description:_____

_____ Rating: ☆☆☆☆☆

Name/Description:_____

_____ Rating: ☆☆☆☆☆

Name/Description:_____

_____ Rating: ☆☆☆☆☆

Name/Description:_____

_____ Rating: ☆☆☆☆☆

Bars & Barks:

Name/Description:_____

_____ Rating: ☆☆☆☆☆

Name/Description:_____

_____ Rating: ☆☆☆☆☆

Name/Description:_____

_____ Rating: ☆☆☆☆☆

Drinks & Others:

Name/Description:_____

_____ Rating: ☆☆☆☆☆

Name/Description:_____

_____ Rating: ☆☆☆☆☆

Notes:

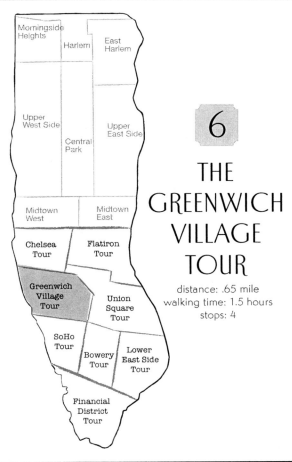

6

THE GREENWICH VILLAGE TOUR

distance: .65 mile
walking time: 1.5 hours
stops: 4

A little over 100 years ago, Greenwich Village was known as "Little Bohemia," a haven for like-minded artists. Though many artists still reside here, the defining characteristic is the labyrinth of streets that can cause bewilderment for residents and tourists alike. In the age of iPhones and GPS systems, you could easily trot your way around, but what's the fun in that? Put aside an afternoon, get lost, and enjoy the adventure that is the "Village." Greenwich village is enclosed north and south by two major streets: 14th Street and Houston Street. Broadway runs on the easterly border, while the Hudson River demarcates the western side. There is no paucity of clothing stores, restaurants, bakeries, or people watching here within this predominantly residential neighborhood.

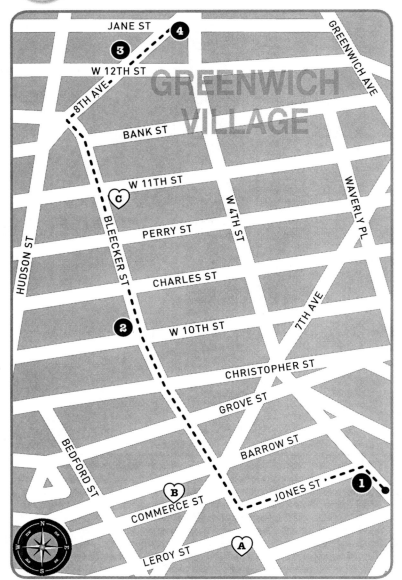

BACK TO THE FUTURE

❶ Varsano's Chocolates:

179 W 4th Street (@ Jones Street)
A West Village location for over 20 years, the hand-dipping expert
Marc Varsano himself will dip anything you can think of into chocolate.

❷ Pure Dark™:

350 Bleecker Street (@ W 10th Street)
The brainchild of the Mars Company, Pure Dark is an experiment
into the world of dark chocolate. Barks, slabs, and trail mix are the
stars here.

❸ Alison Nelson's Chocolate Bar:

19 8th Avenue (between Jane and 12th Streets)
The innovative and energetic Alison Nelson
started in the West Village and is now
expanding into the vast Asian markets.
Check out the funky chocolate bar wrappers.

> In order for chocolate to not feel gritty, the nibs must be crushed to a size below 30 microns. A human hair varies between 50 and 120 microns in thickness.

❹ Li-Lac Chocolates:

40 8th Avenue (@ Jane Street)
Having been around for over 90 years, the
mom-and-pop-inspired Li-Lac knows how to
treat its customers. Martha Bond is only the
fourth owner of this purple-hued village shop.

Greenwich Village LOCAL STOPS

Ⓐ Murray's Cheese Shop:

254 Bleecker Street (@ Leroy Street)
New York City's oldest cheese shop. An absolute must for any
cheese lover. There is also a variety of other imported goods and specialty food items, as
well as cheese-tasting classes.

Ⓑ Milk and Cookies Bakery:

19 Commerce Street (between 7th Avenue and Bedford Street)
This is cookie heaven, folks. You can design your own cookie dough and take it to go.
Choose your add-ins and they will mix it up for you.

Ⓒ Magnolia Bakery:

401 Bleecker Street (@ W 11th Street)
Yes, the cupcakes are definitely worth the wait in line; just make sure you buy enough!
We highly recommend the banana pudding as well.

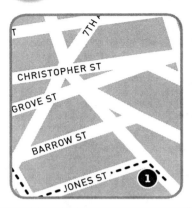

❶ Varsano's Chocolates

179 W 4th Street
New York, NY 10014
212.352.1171
800.414.4718 (phone orders)
varsanos.com

CHOCOLATIER:
Marc Varsano

CHOCOLATE USED:
Varsano uses a proprietary blend of chocolate for his creations.

History:

Marc Varsano, owner and chocolatier of Varsano's, is one of the more jovial people we've met on our chocolate travels. He tells us that he uses a proprietary blend to make his chocolate creations. In short, nobody will be learning his sought-after chocolate secrets at this Greenwich Village institution anytime soon. In fact, the mystery behind Marc Varsano goes far beyond his trade secrets. We were unable to find anything about his personal history, except for the fact that he was a member of the US National Racewalking 20K Team!

All we know is that Varsano has been dedicated to the art of all things chocolate since coming out of college in the mid 1980's. At Varsano's, the chocolate speaks for itself, look no further than to some of the hundreds of positive customer reviews. Here is one we agree with fully:

"Varsano has mastered the art of chocolate tempering, which gives his bars a crisp snap when you break it. The cacao he uses has a wonderful deep and earthy after taste, which is an indication that the beans have been meticuously fermented. We guarantee that your taste buds will be happy, begging you to return for more."

Experience:

West 4th Street is almost always infused with a colorful sensory experience; whether you are people watching or window-shopping, the West Village has a little something for everyone. One of the mainstays in this neighborhood is the charming and homespun character of Varsano's, a village institution since 1986.

After attending college, Marc Varsano, jovial and proud owner, brought his homemade recipes to the public, fortunately for us, he's still going

HOURS:
12pm—7pm every day

SUBWAYS:
A, C, E, B, D, F, M to West 4th Street
1 to Christopher Street/Sheridan Square

SHIPPING:
Worldwide shipping available

strong. Varsano loves his chocolate so much that the very kitchen in which all of the concoctions are created, is literally in the back of the store.

If you are feeling a slight tugging or pulling sensation upon entering Varsano's, no need for concern. It may be the gravitational energy emanating from the Peanut Butter Cups. We haven't denied them yet and don't plan on ever doing so.

The CPR, a pretzel stick coated in caramel and hand-dipped in a smooth chocolate, is heavenly goodness to the last bite. Not to be denied either.

Besides the accommodating and old-fashioned nature of this store, Varsano's also has a stunning array of chocolate-coated objects, from bunnies to cars. These are pre-made, but can also be personalized if that's your wish. Varsano encourages his customers to dream big, claiming that he will dip anything that can be dipped and have it ready for you the following day.

No room for seating here. Grab your chocolate and enjoy the happenings of the West Village.

Greenwich Village **PROFESSOR PICKS**
May we suggest our favorites:
• Chocolate-Covered Caramel Pretzels
• Homemade Peanut Butter Cups

Greenwich Village **BACK TO THE FUTURE**

Varsano's Chocolates Purchases

Truffles & Bonbons:

Name/Description:

Rating: ☆☆☆☆☆

Name/Description:

Rating: ☆☆☆☆☆

Name/Description:

Rating: ☆☆☆☆☆

Name/Description:

Rating: ☆☆☆☆☆

Bars & Barks:

Name/Description:

Rating: ☆☆☆☆☆

Name/Description:

Rating: ☆☆☆☆☆

Name/Description:

Rating: ☆☆☆☆☆

Drinks & Others:

Name/Description:

Rating: ☆☆☆☆☆

Name/Description:

Rating: ☆☆☆☆☆

Notes:

Share your feedback with us @ professorchocolate.com

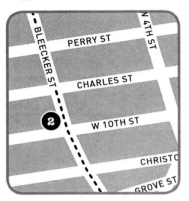

❷ Pure Dark™

350 Bleecker Street
New York, NY 10014
917.284.1927
puredark.com

CHOCOLATIER:
Mars, Inc™

CHOCOLATE USED:
Proprietary blend of premium chocolate beans from West Africa, Dominican Republic, and South America.

History:

For much of the 20th century, the American chocolate scene was dominated by two competing companies: Mars™ and Hershey™. The Mars company makes beloved American confections such as Snickers, M&M's, and Orbit Gum. We are known to chomp on the occasional Snickers or throw back a few M&M's, but with the caveat that it's closer to candy than it is to chocolate. Enter Pure Dark.

Pure Dark is ensconced on a cute and unassuming corner of Bleecker Street in Manhattan's Greenwich Village. According to the spiel that customers receive from a trained employee, Americans have been fixated on milk chocolate for quite some time, so Pure Dark has taken up the task of educating the American consumer about why small-batch dark chocolate is just as good,

and may be even better for you than milk chocolate.

Though Pure Dark is not run by a single chocolatier, the chocolate is handcrafted and unprocessed, certainly with the discerning chocolate consumer in mind. Namely, you.

Experience:

Pure Dark opened in the fall of 2008 with a focus on chocolate education. Truffles and bonbons are not sold here, but don't let this keep

HOURS:
Mon—Thurs: 12pm—7pm
Fri and Sat:11am—8pm
Sun: 11am—6pm

SUBWAYS:
1 to Christopher Street/
Sheridan Square

SHIPPING:
Year-round shipping via FedEx and
USPS within the Unites States.

you away from the exquisite and pristine-like character of Pure Dark. The brown-hued walls and faux cacao trees and pods resembles the interior of a South American rainforest.

There are a couple of different stations or "bars" in Pure Dark, all offering top-shelf chocolate in a variety of ways. For starters, there is the chocolate bark station. This station offers different blends and percentages of cocoa bark with helpful taste tests from willing employees.

Toward the back of Pure Dark, there is another station. This one is devoted to a fun chocolate enterprise: mixing fruits, nuts, and chocolate, which can be bought by the ounce. The trail-like mixes alone are worth the visit to Pure Dark, invigoratingly crunchy from the first to the last handful. Ask for free samples, and the friendly staff will always oblige and educate. Be sure to also try the hot chocolate mixes, but beware! The hot chocolate is very rich and worth sharing with a buddy.

Greenwich Village **PROFESSOR PICKS**
May we suggest our favorites?
• Trail Mix: Pure Dark™ Chocolate-Covered Nibs,
Crystallized Ginger & Pecans
• Chocolate SLAB: Serious Dark Chocolate with
Caramelized Nibs & Coarse Sugar

Pure Dark™ Purchases

Truffles & Bonbons:

Name/Description:

Rating: ☆☆☆☆☆

Name/Description:

Rating: ☆☆☆☆☆

Name/Description:

Rating: ☆☆☆☆☆

Name/Description:

Rating: ☆☆☆☆☆

Bars & Barks:

Name/Description:

Rating: ☆☆☆☆☆

Name/Description:

Rating: ☆☆☆☆☆

Name/Description:

Rating: ☆☆☆☆☆

Drinks & Others:

Name/Description:

Rating: ☆☆☆☆☆

Name/Description:

Rating: ☆☆☆☆☆

BACK TO THE FUTURE

Notes:

Share your feedback with us @ professorchocolate.com

BACK TO THE FUTURE

Greenwich Village

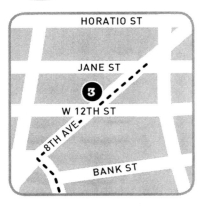

HORATIO ST

JANE ST

3

W 12TH ST

8TH AVE.

BANK ST

3 Alison Nelson's Chocolate Bar

19 8th Avenue
New York, NY 10014
212.366.1541
chocolatebarnyc.com

CHOCOLATIER:
Alison Nelson

CHOCOLATE USED:
· Barry Callebaut
· Equadorian single-origin chocolate
  from Plantation

History:

One of the more fascinating chocolate stories in New York City most certainly radiates from Alison Nelson's Chocolate Bar.

The daughter of a fireman and a caterer, Nelson combines her native New York savviness with unrestrained diligence. Though she does have experience in the private sector, chocolate didn't officially bleep on her radar until about 2000. The initial $75,000 investment in 2002 marked the beginning of the Chocolate Bar and Nelson's debut into the wide world of chocolate.

Over the next few years, Nelson became immersed in the business of making and selling chocolate. One of her claims to fame is her fashion-forward chocolate-bar packaging, which features renderings of funky graffiti and designs, created by local artists.

These arty designs caught the

eye of the Dubai-based company, HFK General Trading. HFK approached Nelson about expanding her brand in exotic locations such as Qatar and the United Arab Emirates. Seizing the opportunity of a lifetime, Nelson signed on.

Her growing Chocolate Bar brand is now projected to reach 30 locations, most of it being slated for the Middle East and other parts of Asia, like India and Pakistan. These countries are seen as "virgin soil" for the highly specialized food niche that is being quickly occupied by more and more entrepreneurs.

All the meanwhile, Chocolate Bar NYC had moved from its original Greenwich Village location to the Lower East Side, then back again to its current spot on 8th Avenue. Not to worry, Nelson just recently signed a 10-year lease, so when you go hunting for Miss Nelson and her artist-in-

Mon—Fri: 7:30am—10pm
Sat and Sun: 8:30am—10pm

SUBWAYS:
A, C, E to 14th Street
L to 8th Avenue

SHIPPING:
Most orders shipped the next business day via UPS.

spired chocolate, they'll be there.

Experience:

Occupying a sweet and unpretentious spot in the middle of the block, Alison Nelson's Chocolate Bar draws everyone from foot-trafficking locals to planned chocolate tours. Shelves are stacked with her scintillating chocolate bars, wrapped in ultra-funky designer paper. Truffles and bonbons are displayed toward the front, accompanying Barrington Coffee and freshly baked cookies and treats. The joint itself is low-key and peaceful.

From the atmosphere to the packaging to the chocolate itself, the whole package of what you see at Alison Nelson's Chocolate Bar is the formula that is being replicated in the far-off corners of the world. How very exciting that it all started right here in the Village.

Greenwich Village — BACK TO THE FUTURE

Alison Nelson's Chocolate Bar Purchases

Truffles & Bonbons:

Name/Description:

Rating: ☆☆☆☆☆

Name/Description:

Rating: ☆☆☆☆☆

Name/Description:

Rating: ☆☆☆☆☆

Name/Description:

Rating: ☆☆☆☆☆

Bars & Barks:

Name/Description:

Rating: ☆☆☆☆☆

Name/Description:

Rating: ☆☆☆☆☆

Name/Description:

Rating: ☆☆☆☆☆

Drinks & Others:

Name/Description:

Rating: ☆☆☆☆☆

Name/Description:

Rating: ☆☆☆☆☆

Notes:

Share your feedback with us @ professorchocolate.com

❹ Li-Lac Chocolates

40 8th Avenue
New York, NY 10014
212.924.2280
718.567.9500 (phone orders)
li-lacchocolates.com

CHOCOLATIER:
Martha Bond

CHOCOLATE USED:
· Peter's Chocolate

History:

In 1923, George Demetrious started Li-Lac Chocolates with a most delectable and treasured, small-batch truffle recipe. Eighty-seven years later and Li-Lac is still drawing customers both old and new. Christopher Street was the original location of Li-Lac for most of those years, and it wasn't until 2005 when Martha Bond, the current owner, was forced to move Li-Lac to its present street-crossing location of Jane Street, West 4th Street, and 8th Avenue.

Bond is just the fourth owner in the almost 90 years of the shop's life. Most of that time Li-Lac was owned and operated by Demetrious, who died in 1972. Before his death, he passed his coveted chocolate recipes and shop to a loyal employee of 25 years, Marguerite Watt. Watt maintained the high standard of chocolate-making and customer service for

five years before she entrusted the business onto local caterer, friend, and frequent visitor, Edward Bond.

In 1981, Martha Bond, Ed's sister, joined her brother in the chocolate-making business and has been the chocolatier since 1990. Martha remains loyal to many of the techniques and recipes that have been passed down from Demetrious, and she even expanded the business to Grand Central Terminal. In its 10th decade of business, Li-Lac continues to make chocolate that simply makes people smile.

Experience:

Entering Li-Lac is like stepping into an oasis of tranquility. Everything here just seems happy. Maybe it starts with the lavender walls or the aroma of freshly made chocolate and fudge. The smiling employees talking with customers on a first-name basis

Greenwich Village BACK TO THE FUTURE

HOURS:
Mon—Sat: 12pm—8pm
Sun: 12pm—5pm

SUBWAYS:
L to 8th Ave.

SHIPPING:
Overnight, second-day, and ground shipping are available. Same-day delivery in Manhattan also available.

makes us feel that we should visit more often. Li-Lac also serves up a hefty helping of old-fashioned hospitality with its enticing chocolate.

If you are looking for posh bonbons and truffles with sexy names, you need not look here. The mom-and-pop establishment does however have a substantial collection of hand-dipped chocolate classics. You name it, and it's hand-dipped and in the display case. All chocolates are made on demand with only the freshest ingredients. There are a handful of truffles and bonbons available, including boozy favorites such as rum and amaretto and the award-winning Raspberry Truffle created by current

owner, Martha Bond.

One of the most popular items here could be the fudge that's made from scratch. No pre-made mixes are used, just pure and fresh ingredients, and indulging customers know it too, they come from far and wide.

Traditional flavors plus old-fashioned dipping methods make LiLac not only a favorite among many New Yorkers, but a clear front-runner as a New York institution that treats its customers like family. Your taste buds and feelings will thank you for this stopover.

Greenwich Village PROFESSOR PICKS

May we suggest our favorites?
• Raspberry Truffles
• Legendary Homemade Fudge

Li-Lac Chocolates
Purchases

Truffles & Bonbons:

Name/Description: _____

Rating: ☆☆☆☆☆

Name/Description: _____

Rating: ☆☆☆☆☆

Name/Description: _____

Rating: ☆☆☆☆☆

Name/Description: _____

Rating: ☆☆☆☆☆

Bars & Barks:

Name/Description: _____

Rating: ☆☆☆☆☆

Name/Description: _____

Rating: ☆☆☆☆☆

Name/Description: _____

Rating: ☆☆☆☆☆

Drinks & Others:

Name/Description: _____

Rating: ☆☆☆☆☆

Name/Description: _____

Rating: ☆☆☆☆☆

Notes:

Share your feedback with us @ professorchocolate.com

7

THE CHELSEA TOUR

distance: .70 mile
walking time: 2 hours
stops: 4

Chelsea is nestled between the cheap eats of Hell's Kitchen to the north and the hip eateries and nightlife of the Meatpacking District to its south. Home to many photographers and artists who, in the last 20 years, have found a home in Chelsea for their modern works of art. Though this neighborhood is now quite the fashionable one, it didn't use to be so. In fact, it wasn't long ago that the longshoreman who worked the docks inhabited this part of town. Factories and even a railroad (now the Elevated High Line Park) were erected during times of major industry. Elegant brownstones line quiet streets, making excellent scenery for a Sunday afternoon stroll.

Chelsea HIGH LINE PICNIC

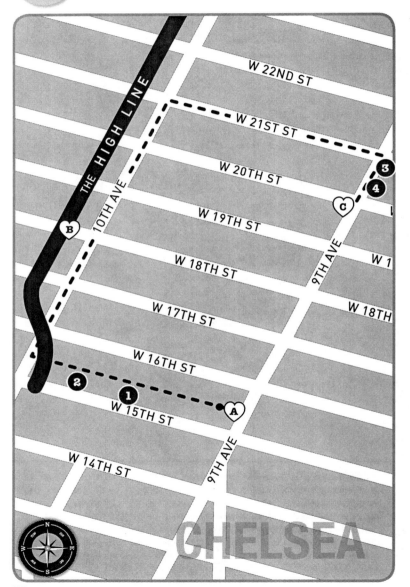

Chelsea HIGH LINE PICNIC

1 Jacques Torres (at Chelsea Market):
75 9th Avenue (between 9th and 10th Avenues)
This location at the Chelsea Market is like a dream within a dream.
There is a full selection of products at this location, including some of
our favorites: Chocolate-covered Cheerios and Cornflakes.

2 Chelsea Market Baskets:
75 9th Avenue (In Chelsea Market near 10th Avenue)
Flooded with both natives and tourists, the Chelsea Market is one of
New York's best places to forage for anything from chocolate and
sweets to meats and wine. The vintage architecture is a treat unto itself.
CMB will help you keep it all together and share the experience with
anyone, anywhere in the country.

3 Cocoa V Chocolat:
174 9th Avenue (between 21st and 22nd Streets)
The northern-most shop on this tour, Cocoa V specializes in all vegan
chocolates and treats. Serves breakfast, lunch, and tea as well.

4 Three Tarts:
164 9th Avenue (@ 20th Street)
The nickname given to three very talented women in pastry school
stuck. Now they own their own boutique to show off all of the elegant
giftware and savory sweets.

Chelsea LOCAL STOPS

A Chelsea Market:
75 9th Avenue (between 15th and 16th Streets)
Create your perfect picnic basket as you stroll
through this post-industrial theme park interspersed
with fine food stores and restaurants.

B The High Line:
*Elevator access @ 14th and 16th Streets
(near 10th Avenue)*
The High Line was originally constructed in the
'30s to lift dangerous freight trains off Manhattan's
streets. Completely redesigned and renovated, this
elevated park is now open to the public. A great
spot for a picnic.

C La Bergamote Patisserie:
169 9th Ave (@ 20th Street)
The fact that they are considered by some to have
the best croissants in the city only adds to the
appeal of its chocolate-infused pastries.

Cacao trees grow
in areas 20° to the
North and South of the
equator where the average
temperature and
humidity are high.

W 17TH ST
W 16TH ST
W 15TH ST
W 14TH ST
9TH AVE

❶ Jacques Torres
(at Chelsea Market)
75 9th Avenue
New York, NY 10011
212.414.2462
mrchocolate.com

CHOCOLATIER:
Jacques Torres

CHOCOLATE USED:
Jacques is one of the few chocolatiers who can produce his own chocolate from the bean. He even uses fully restored vintage equipment.

History:

About 10 years ago, the famed pastry chef, Jacques Torres, decided to make his own chocolate for quality control purposes. This is a huge undertaking, and one that proved to be a successful venture. Certainly a testament to the will and ingenuity of Torres.

Originally, he never intended to welcome visitors; he situated his factory in a somewhat remote section of Brooklyn called D.U.M.B.O. (Down Under the Manhattan Bridge Overpass) because rent was cheap.

Legend has it that Jacques renovated much of the store himself using a pastry bag and an off-set spatula to pipe out and smooth caulk and cement just like icing on a cake.

The first day that the store opened, with an empty shoebox for a cash register, Jacques started selling his chocolates. The rest, is history (no pun intended).

When he first made truffles, Jacques blended Valrhona Manjari and a 70% chocolate but was disappointed with the results. Now, Jacques uses his own neutral 60% blend, which allows the flavors in the truffles to explode before you taste the chocolate.

According to Jacques, he hasn't changed his recipes, but he has refined his techniques. One secret was vacuuming all the air out of his ganache (truffle or bonbon filling). That way, the aromas won't evaporate. Cumulatively, his secrets have helped him to become one of the most prominent chocolate personalities in the world.

Experience:

The selection and confluence of high-end food and desserts at Chelsea Market may be unrivaled in New York City. The 800-foot-long corridor of Chelsea Market is not only a place

Chelsea HIGH LINE PICNIC

HOURS:
Mon—Sat: 7am—10pm
Sun: 8am—8pm

SUBWAYS:
A, C, E to 14th Street
L to 8th Avenue

SHIPPING:
Year-round shipping with FedEx.
Monday through Thursday overnight
available.

ADDITIONAL INFO:
Chocolate of the Month Club
available.

where you can truly explore for food, but it is also a museum of industrial relics leftover from the turn of the last century. Be sure to check out the walls, ceiling, floors, and outcroppings of various remnants, all full of character and charm.

The actual foundation of this building was built in the mid-19th century, with its primary claim to fame being that it was the site of the Nabisco baking factory. The baking ovens remained hot for much of the early part of the 20th century, creating the classic Oreo cookie in 1913. The later part of the 20th century brought with it an emphasis on industry and, eventually,

neglect. According to the Chelsea Market website, the '70s and '80s have no record of any bakery on the premises. A renaissance of sorts was started in the mid '90s, when a firm renovated the present foodie paradise corridor that runs east to west between 9th and 10th Avenues.

Jacques Torres can be found about midway down the long corridor on the south side. That would be the left-hand side coming from 9th Ave. It shares a large, divided common space with several other tantalizing shops such as Gramercy Flower Shop, One Lucky Duck, People's Pops, Lucy's Whey, and Nutbox.

 Chelsea **PROFESSOR PICKS**

May we suggest our favorites?
• Chocolate-covered Cheerios and Cornflakes
• Hot Chocolate (made with real chocolate, not cocoa powder)
• Almondine Truffles

Chelsea HIGH LINE PICNIC

Jacques Torres at Chelsea Market Purchases

Truffles & Bonbons:

Name/Description:

Rating: ☆☆☆☆☆

Name/Description:

Rating: ☆☆☆☆☆

Name/Description:

Rating: ☆☆☆☆☆

Name/Description:

Rating: ☆☆☆☆☆

Bars & Barks:

Name/Description:

Rating: ☆☆☆☆☆

Name/Description:

Rating: ☆☆☆☆☆

Name/Description:

Rating: ☆☆☆☆☆

Drinks & Others:

Name/Description:

Rating: ☆☆☆☆☆

Name/Description:

Rating: ☆☆☆☆☆

Chelsea HIGH LINE PICNIC

Notes:

Share your feedback with us @ professorchocolate.com

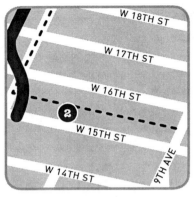

❷ Chelsea Market Baskets

75 9th Avenue
New York, NY 10011
888.727.7887
212.727.1111
chelseamarketbaskets.com

CHOCOLATIER:
Multiple chocolatiers stock their
finest products at the store

History:

As a young man in Provincetown, Massachusetts, David Porat once cooked a meal for Julia Child and her husband. As a businessman, he spent 13 years in corporate retailing as a buyer and product manager for Bloomingdale's and Macy's. In 1993, he started out on his own as a food broker, doing business primarily in wholesale and mail-order gift baskets. Four years later, Porat signed a 20-year lease for his shop in the Chelsea Market food mall, then being developed by building owner Irwin Cohen.

Presently, a 28,000 square-foot warehouse in New Jersey receives imported goods by the container. He and his staff of 60 employees have the ability to ship up to 1,000 baskets each day.

Chelsea Market Baskets is deservingly the main inspiration for the title of this tour. Whether you are picking up a premade basket or creating a custom basket, it is sure to be filled with specialty goods

from around the world. The store houses one of the more impressive chocolate displays that we know of in Manhattan.

For us, knowing that there is a giant display case of Leonidas Chocolates, and a side selection of other fine chocolates from around the world, is more than enough reason to stock up for a High Line picnic. As a matter of fact, Chelsea Market Baskets is the largest U.S. wholesale customer of imported Leonidas chocolate.

One of the only "problems" we can think of is that if you are the type of person to wildly tear into your presents, the expertly presented baskets may betray your instincts. They are almost as decadent to look at as they are to open and enjoy. In addition to Leonidas, CMB also hosts a series of somewhat new artisanal American chocolatiers, incorporating fair trade principles and single estate chocolates to produce their confections. Some of these include: Fran's Salted Caramels, which are on President Obama's shortlist.

Chelsea HIGH LINE PICNIC

HOURS:
Mon—Fri: 9:30am—8pm
Sat: 10am—8pm
Sun: 10am—6pm

SUBWAYS:
A, C, E to 14th Street
L to 8th Avenue

SHIPPING:
Shipping is available Monday through Friday via UPS in the U.S. only. Same-day messenger service in Manhattan, including weekends.

ADDITIONAL INFO:
Order baskets by 3pm and allow three hours before picking up. After 3pm, baskets will be ready by 11am the following morning.

Berkshire Bark from Massachusetts, Marie-Belle's Aztec Hot Chocolate, Fat Witch Brownies, Mast Brothers Chocolate, and CMB's own Chocolate Bar.

Experience:

Few neighborhoods in New York have seen as dramatic a turnaround as the western edge of Chelsea. This turnaround can almost solely be attributed to the development of the Chelsea Market food mall by building owner Irwin Cohen.

Cohen approached the David Porat and other local wholesalers of quality food about opening retail outlets in the ground floor space of an 11-story building with the Meatpacking District on one side and the High Line hovering on the other. It has become a smorgasbord of food and other shops as well as being the official home of The Food Network. For decades, the structure was part of the Nabisco™ bakeries, churning out Fig Newtons, Animal Crackers, Oreos and Mallomars. These cookies have been replaced by artisan cookies and cupcakes, not such a bad thing. The indoor market, occupying the block from 9th to 10th Avenues offers an array of restaurants and specialty food stores.

Remnants of the old architecture and dazzling sculptures are present throughout the entire space. Be sure to visit Chelsea Market Baskets and the potpourri of stores which await you.

Chelsea PROFESSOR PICKS
May we suggest our favorites?
• Leonidas Truffle Speculoos
• Smoked Salt Caramels from Fran's Chocolates

Chelsea **HIGH LINE PICNIC**

Chelsea Market Baskets
Purchases

Truffles & Bonbons:

Name/Description:

Rating: ☆☆☆☆☆

Name/Description:

Rating: ☆☆☆☆☆

Name/Description:

Rating: ☆☆☆☆☆

Name/Description:

Rating: ☆☆☆☆☆

Bars & Barks:

Name/Description:

Rating: ☆☆☆☆☆

Name/Description:

Rating: ☆☆☆☆☆

Name/Description:

Rating: ☆☆☆☆☆

Drinks & Others:

Name/Description:

Rating: ☆☆☆☆☆

Name/Description:

Rating: ☆☆☆☆☆

Chelsea HIGH LINE PICNIC

Notes:

Share your feedback with us @ professorchocolate.com

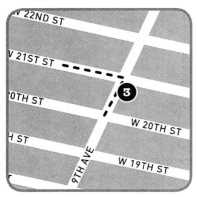

❸ Cocoa V Chocolat
174 9th Avenue
New York, NY 10011
212.242.3339
cocoav.com

CHOCOLATIER:
Patrick Coston

CHOCOLATE USED:
Organic, vegan, fair-trade beans
grown in the Dominican Republic
and processed in Switzerland

History:

In 2006, Pamela Blackwell opened Blossom Restaurant & Cafe, her first restaurant specializing in vegan cuisine. Three years later, she met a talented chocolatier who matched her penchant and passion for vegan treats, and they opened Cocoa V.

The driving philosophy behind Cocoa V is to beget healthy and scrumptious-tasting chocolate. The cacao beans themselves are harvested in the Dominican Republic, sent to Switzerland for processing, and then forwarded to the whimsical hands of chocolatier Patrick Coston. Above all else is Cocoa V's all-vegan philosophy for artisanal chocolates, handcrafted in the on-site kitchen.

Coston has had an illustrious career that spans back and forth from San Franciso, Las Vegas, and New York. Pastry Art & Design magazine recognized him as one of America's top 10 pastry chefs in back-to-back years in 2002 and 2003.

Not only does Cocoa V create a preciously-good line of chocolate products, it also focuses on creation with a conscience. Underlying the all-vegan line of tasty treats is a precise execution to avoid hurting any animals during the process of making the goods sold at Cocoa V. This includes avoiding dairy products. It has become common practice these days for dairy cows to be pushed to their limits to sustain a steady stream of milk, leading to inhumane treatment. Cocoa V eschews this altogether, and still manages to delight our taste buds.

Experience:

Less than two blocks away from the High Line elevated park is a highly experienced pastry chef and chocolatier with a truly unique product. Patrick Coston goes above and beyond to create a chocolates that are highly specialized, yet delectable.

Chelsea HIGH LINE PICNIC

HOURS:
(Seasonal)
Mon: 4pm—9pm
Tue—Wed: 12pm—9pm
Thurs: 12pm—10pm
Fri: 12:pm—10:30pm
Sat: 10:30am—10:30pm
Sun: 12pm—8pm

SUBWAYS:
A, C, E to 14th Street
C, E to 23rd Street

SHIPPING:
Year-round shipping via FedEx and
USPS within the U.S.

ADDITIONAL INFO:
All items are organic, fair trade, and
vegan.

Every treat in the shop is made onsite, never too far away from Coston and his staff.

According to their website, they are the first "100% vegan, organic, fair-trade chocolate shop to date" in the city. No dairy products here.

One of our favorite morsels here is the naturally sweet, yet not-too-sweet Agave bonbon, always on display and available on the website as well. A most delicious take-home treat is the Roasted Edamame Cluster, which is soaked in a velvety vegan chocolate.

Besides creating a unique and all-vegan stash, Cocoa V also serves small and inviting meals and snacks. All-vegan specials such as nut cheeses paired with

wine, smoothies, and quiches round out a very healthy and exciting menu. The Professors frequently visit to enjoy the ever-expanding selection of toothsome treats.

 Chelsea **PROFESSOR PICKS**
May we suggest our favorites?
• Stumptown Coffee Caramel Bonbons
• Roasted Edamame Clusters

Cocoa V Chocolat
Purchases

Truffles & Bonbons:

Name/Description:

Rating: ☆☆☆☆☆

Name/Description:

Rating: ☆☆☆☆☆

Name/Description:

Rating: ☆☆☆☆☆

Name/Description:

Rating: ☆☆☆☆☆

Bars & Barks:

Name/Description:

Rating: ☆☆☆☆☆

Name/Description:

Rating: ☆☆☆☆☆

Name/Description:

Rating: ☆☆☆☆☆

Drinks & Others:

Name/Description:

Rating: ☆☆☆☆☆

Name/Description:

Rating: ☆☆☆☆☆

Chelsea HIGH LINE PICNIC

Notes:

Share your feedback with us @ professorchocolate.com

❹ Three Tarts

164 9th Avenue
New York, NY 10011
212.462.4392
threetarts.com

CHOCOLATE USED:
· Chocovic
· Barry Callebaut
· Noel
· Valrhona

History:

Three Tarts is the sobriquet given to three very talented female pastry chefs during their time at the Institute for Culinary Education, or I.C.E of NYC. Marla D'urso, Sandra Palmer, and Kiyomi Todo-Burke made their school-time moniker official business in 2006. The trinity's members each hone in on a specific set of pastry fine-tuning, benefitting the palates of any customer.

Marla D'urso is founder and listed as the "head tart." It is she who captures the essence of interior design, love of pastry, and knack for keeping the place spotless.

Kiyomi Toda-Burke's resumé includes working for venerable restaurants and pastry chefs in New York City. Her pastry skills and creative propensity stem from her years as a fashion designer. All of the bite-size treats look as good as they do due to her gifted hands.

Inside Sandra Palmer's pastry chef toolkit is an obsession for making things right, which is most likely why she is the kitchen manager. She too graduated from I.C.E. of New York City and brings with her a considerable talent for the kinds of pastries that you will soon devour.

If you've skipped the profile of each woman and simply want the bottom line, ponder over this quote from the Three Tarts website: "We are obsessed with the art of giving. We bring together two sweet things—masterfully crafted desserts made from the finest ingredients and an eclectic, hand-picked selection of giftware."

Experience:

On one of our recent visits to Three Tarts, it happened to be a chilly and rain-soaked Saturday afternoon. As unfriendly as the weather was that day, Three Tarts was as warm and inviting as a tiny coun-

Chelsea HIGH LINE PICNIC

try store tucked away in "anywhere" USA. Upon entering, we were greeted with soft music, the scent of freshly baked goods, and a warm smile by one of the employees.

A small retail area of elegant giftware complements the baked goods at Three Tarts, but make no mistake, the bite-size tarts, cookies, petits fours, brownies made with Valrhona Chocolate, and chocolate truffles are the highlight of this petite boutique. The displayed treats for the most part, are pocket-sized and adorable, making us feel like we should start a collection of everything Three Tarts.

Everything edible here is made in the back kitchen by one of the uber-talented women, including the multi-flavored gourmet marshmallows and the seasonal favorite, a homemade version of Peeps! Also crafted on-site are the hand-made caramel sea salt truffles, perfectly shaped for a tasty, and a not too chewy, hair-tickling experience. Other truffle flavors include ginger, lavender, and classic dark.

Prolonged exposure to Three Tarts only decreases blood pressure and increases joy and tranquility, so be sure to grab one of the three tiny tables for two.

 Chelsea PROFESSOR PICKS
May we suggest our favorites?
•Lemon Coconut Yumballs and Petits Fours
• Dark Rolled Truffles

Chelsea **HIGH LINE PICNIC**

Three Tarts
Purchases

Truffles & Bonbons:

Name/Description:

Rating: ☆☆☆☆☆

Name/Description:

Rating: ☆☆☆☆☆

Name/Description:

Rating: ☆☆☆☆☆

Name/Description:

Rating: ☆☆☆☆☆

Bars & Barks:

Name/Description:

Rating: ☆☆☆☆☆

Name/Description:

Rating: ☆☆☆☆☆

Name/Description:

Rating: ☆☆☆☆☆

Drinks & Others:

Name/Description:

Rating: ☆☆☆☆☆

Name/Description:

Rating: ☆☆☆☆☆

Notes:

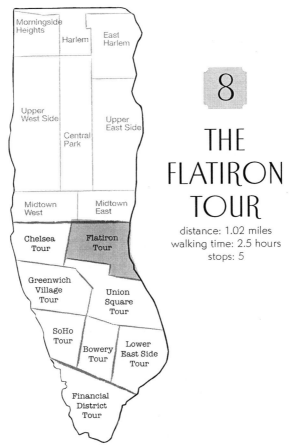

8

THE
FLATIRON
TOUR

distance: 1.02 miles
walking time: 2.5 hours
stops: 5

As recently as the mid-1980s, the area known as the Flatiron District was known as the Photo District. Cheap rents had attracted photographers who occupied much-needed studio space. Now, real-estate isn't so cheap and the Flatiron District, named so after one of the more famous architectural buildings in Manhattan, is a haven for restaurants and high-end residential living. Broadway slices through the middle of the Flatiron District, leading one right to Madison Square Park and its serene setting; while 6th Avenue and Lexington Avenue hedge the eastern and western perimeter of the Flatiron.

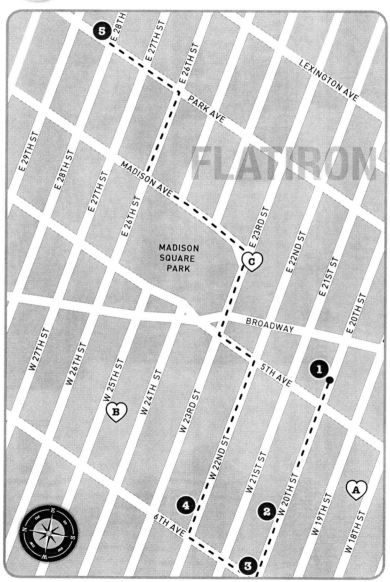

Flatiron COCOATASTIC TOUR

1 L.A. Burdick:
5 E 20th Street (between 5th Avenue and Broadway)
Cozy and enchanting, the New England-based boutique has opened up shop in the Flatiron District. Adorable chocolate mice and a smooth hot chocolate are Burdick's signature creations.

2 Chocolat Moderne:
27 W 20th Street, Suite 904 (between 5th and 6th Avenues)
The self-taught Joan Coukos creates her otherworldly chocolates in a 9th floor loft, now kitchen. You'll know you've struck gold when you first enter this treasure trove of artisanal chocolates.

3 MarieBelle (at Limelight Marketplace):
656 6th Avenue (@ 20th Street)
The complete line, and charm, of MarieBelle chocolates are on display. Be sure to check-out the balcony-perched spot. Just look up!

4 L'atelier du chocolat:
59 W 22nd Street (@ 6th Avenue)
Do not be deceived by the closet-size shop. Eric Girerd has been con-cocting chocolate and pastries the world over since the 1970s.

5 FIKA espresso bar:
407 Park Avenue South (@ 28th Street)
Fika is the Swedish verb meaning to "take a coffee break followed by a sweet treat." FIKA takes this to a whole new level with Master Choco-latier Håkan Mårtensson creating lusciously good chocolate.

> Cocoa's taste is partly created by the heating of chemicals formed during the fermentation of the beans. Roasting the beans then further develops the flavor.

Flatiron LOCAL STOPS

A City Bakery: *3 W 18th Street (between 5th and 6th Avenues)*
With a small "chocolate room" stocked with chocolate by both Chocolat Moderne and Bond Street Chocolates, irresistible baked goods, and some of the best hot cocoa in town, we're naming this institution our top favorite.

B Bruce's Best Chocolate: *40 W 25th Street (between Broadway and 6th Avenue)*
Proceed down to the café to find the chocolate creations of Bruce Best, a noted New York City cooking teacher and food writer.

C Bonobo: *18 E 23rd Street (@ Madison Avenue)*
Bonobos are great apes that are 99% genetically similar to us. Their diet is predominantly raw, wild, and plant based: fruits, vegetables, nuts, and seeds, just like the delicious food at this restaurant. We love the coconut chai.

Flatiron COCOATASTIC TOUR

❶ L.A. Burdick

5 E 20th Street
New York, NY 10003
212.796.0143
burdickchocolate.com

CHOCOLATIERS:
Larry Burdick and Michael Klug

CHOCOLATE USED:
· Grenada Chocolate Company
(Couverture, block chocolate, and
chocolate liquor processed in France,
Switzerland, and Venezuela)

History:

Larry Burdick began making chocolate confections in 1984 for a small number of New York City restaurants. A few years later, L.A. Burdick chocolates officially arrived on the scene, expanding its already blooming production line. In the early '90s, the Burdick family, which includes his wife Paula and two kids, moved out of New York and settled in Walpole, NH. Walpole not only became the home of the Burdick family, but also L.A. Burdick's headquarters and the present site of a bistro-style restaurant, inspired by Larry and Paula's time together in France.

Opened in the fall of 2009, the Flatiron location marked the return of L.A. Burdick to New York after a 20-year hiatus. It is the third and most recent of the family of boutique shops (another is located in Cambridge, MA). Though Larry oversees much of the daily operations of the business, head pastry chef and chocolatier Michael Klug performs most of the chocolatiering. Since 2002 the native German has been dedicated to L.A. Burdick and its signature petite bonbons, a combination of complex flavors, textures, and the very best ingredients.

Still wanting more? There are week-long summer chocolate courses available at the Burdick headquarters in Walpole, NH. Here, one can be schooled in art of chocolate-making by Klug himself. You get to keep the chocolates, too!

We have also heard whispers that Burdick is attempting to install and open his very own chocolate processing plant in Grenada. The future certainly bolds well.

Flatiron COCOATASTIC TOUR

HOURS:
Mon–Thur: 9am–9pm
Fri–Sat: 9am–10pm
Sun: 9am–8pm

SUBWAYS:
6 to 23rd Street
F, M to 23rd Street
N, R to 23rd Street

SHIPPING:
Orders received before 5pm ship
same-day via FedEx or UPS.

ADDITIONAL INFO:
No preservatives, extracts,
concentrates, or flavorings used.

Experience:

New England charm, that's what first comes to mind when you enter L.A. Burdick's brand-new digs in the Flatiron District. Warm and wooded tones of brown, tranquil lighting, and a friendly staff all combine for a truly outstanding chocolate experience. Plenty of seats accompany the New Hampshire based chocolatier, along with an espresso bar and fresh pastries.

Burdick's signature product comes in the form of scrumptious chocolate mice, never too filling and always a crowd pleaser. To suit all tastes, they are made with dark, milk, or white chocolate with a variety of tasty interiors. The silk tail, however, is not edible. Though the chocolate mice are Burdick's claim to fame, the hot chocolate is masterful. The hot chocolate, or iced hot chocolate, has never left a chalky taste in our mouths nor has it ever bloated our tummies. It is simply the perfect recipe for hot chocolate.

Burdick's bonbons swim in the hearts and minds of many. From classic flavors to cutting-edge options, Burdick is simply a brand that is endearing to the palate of many.

Flatiron COCOATASTIC TOUR

L.A. Burdick
Purchases

Truffles & Bonbons:

Name/Description: _____

_____ Rating: ☆☆☆☆☆

Name/Description: _____

_____ Rating: ☆☆☆☆☆

Name/Description: _____

_____ Rating: ☆☆☆☆☆

Name/Description: _____

_____ Rating: ☆☆☆☆☆

Bars & Barks:

Name/Description: _____

_____ Rating: ☆☆☆☆☆

Name/Description: _____

_____ Rating: ☆☆☆☆☆

Name/Description: _____

_____ Rating: ☆☆☆☆☆

Drinks & Others:

Name/Description: _____

_____ Rating: ☆☆☆☆☆

Name/Description: _____

_____ Rating: ☆☆☆☆☆

Flatiron COCOATASTIC TOUR

Notes:

_____
_____
_____
_____
_____
_____
_____
_____
_____
_____
_____
_____
_____

Share your feedback with us @ professorchocolate.com

❷ Chocolat Moderne

27 W 20th Street, Suite 904
New York, NY 10011
212.229.4797
chocolatmoderne.com

CHOCOLATIER:
Joan Coukos

CHOCOLATE USED:
· Valrhona

History:

During the mid-90s, Joan Coukos was divvying up time between Moscow and Wall Street, enmeshed in the world of finance. She had an MBA from UNC Chapel Hill, with no background in the art of making chocolate. Then came a vacation in 2000 to Brussels. She paid homage to the famed Place du Grand Sablon, an epicenter for specialty chocolate and other precious wares. The experience at the Grand Sablon altered her life and career, chocolate became her passion.

Upon her return to the United States, she was inspired to craft little chocolate treats out of her Manhattan kitchen and feed a handful of happy colleagues. One of the blueprints for becoming a successful chocolatier seems to involve the at-home kitchen/laboratory which soon becomes a small chocolate facility,

followed by accolades and a solid base of consumers like us. In Coukos's story, 2003 marked the official lift off for Chocolat Moderne.

Besides crafting distinctive chocolate and aesthetically-seductive packaging, Food & Wine acknowledged Coukos as one of America's "most exciting chocolate innovators." Just as exciting may be the mini-pilgrimage one has to take to find Coukos. The 9th floor loft is a one-of-a-kind chocolate destination.

Experience:

The New York City experience of finding chocolatiers and their hideaways remains unrivaled thanks in part to shops like Joan Coukos's Chocolat Moderne. Located on a high floor in a nondescript building, Chocolat Moderne can be just as fun to get to as it is eating the chocolate. Well, almost.

Flatiron COCOATASTIC TOUR

HOURS:
Please call ahead if you plan to stop by as this shop does not have a traditional storefront.

SUBWAYS:
F, M to 23rd Street
N, R to 23rd Street

SHIPPING:
Chocolates shipped within three business days of ordering via FedEx. Same-day messenger service in Manhattan.

ADDITIONAL INFO:
No preservatives or artificial flavors used.

Check for hours of operation before you make the trek. Believe us when we tell you that it will be well worth the effort. Once you enter the loft space through cocoa-toned doors, the aroma of chocolate and racks of truffles and bars await you. Tempting as it may be to choose your chocolate and go, stay and mingle with Coukos or one of her delightful staff members.

We have been lucky enough on a few occasions to be on the receiving end of sumptuous bar and bonbon samples. Bursting with flavor and intensity is Chocolat Moderne's Japanese-inspired Kimono Collection. Bonbons are infused with unique in-gredients such as shiso leaf, adzuki bean paste, and macha green tea. Our favorite? The Soy-Miso. It has homemade caramel with tamari soy and white miso paste. One bite and you'll be donning your own kimono and dancing your way to cherry-blossom land.

 Flatiron PROFESSOR PICKS

May we suggest our favorites?
•Soy-Miso Truffles from the Kimono Collection
• Chocolat Moderne Sea Salt Bars

Chocolat Moderne
Purchases

Truffles & Bonbons:

Name/Description:_____

_____ Rating: ☆☆☆☆☆

Name/Description:_____

_____ Rating: ☆☆☆☆☆

Name/Description:_____

_____ Rating: ☆☆☆☆☆

Name/Description:_____

_____ Rating: ☆☆☆☆☆

Bars & Barks:

Name/Description:_____

_____ Rating: ☆☆☆☆☆

Name/Description:_____

_____ Rating: ☆☆☆☆☆

Name/Description:_____

_____ Rating: ☆☆☆☆☆

Drinks & Others:

Name/Description:_____

_____ Rating: ☆☆☆☆☆

Name/Description:_____

_____ Rating: ☆☆☆☆☆

Flatiron COCOATASTIC TOUR

Notes:

Share your feedback with us @ professorchocolate.com

Flatiron COCOATASTIC TOUR

❸ MarieBelle
(at Limelight Marketplace)
656 6th Avenue
New York, NY 10011
212.925.6999 (MarieBelle)
212.226.7585 (Limelight Marketplace)
mariebelle.com

CHOCOLATIER:
Maribel Lieberman

CHOCOLATE USED:
· Barry Callebaut

History:

At the corner of 6th avenue and 20th street, the first brick of the Holy Communion Church was laid in 1844. Over 130 years later, the church building was bought out by a company that used the space for a drug and counseling center. By 1983, the holy grounds had been acquired yet again, but this time converted to the clubbing mecca, Limelight. Andy Warhol hosted the rollicking opening night party, and it remained a Manhattan hotspot for the next 20 years.

A few years of disrepair followed, but that was then and this is 2010. The newly renovated Limelight is now the site of about 50 upscale shops. From clothing to home goods to accessories, it's one-stop shopping.

Most exciting is the presence of MarieBelle Chocolates (flagship store is in SoHo). It wasn't very long ago that MarieBelle was selling its edible-art confections at the corner of Prince and Mott, but it was the Aztec Hot Chocolate that may have put them on the map. MarieBelle is a deserving recipient of the "Oprah Bump." So much influence did this have, that lines for their precious hot chocolate snaked around the corner of the once little-known MarieBelle.

Experience:

In all of the shops we have searched, found, and profiled, not one place can lay claim to being housed in an old church. The nightclubbing Limelight of the '80s and '90s, once a house of worship, was a dark labyrinth of sneaky stairways and dimly lit corners.

Though some of the maze-like qualities of the club are retained, the multi-level 12,000 square-foot space is brightly lit and modernized. Every

HOURS:
Mon—Sat: 10am—10pm
Sun: 11am—8pm

SUBWAYS:
F, M to 23rd Street
N, R to 23rd Street

SHIPPING:
Same-day delivery via messenger available in Manhattan. FedEx is the preferred shipping method. Shipments go out Monday through Thursday.

few feet walked, we encountered more and more of the site's 50 vendors. From fresh and local veggies to a leather goods store, there's a little something for all.

MarieBelle's luxurious chocolates and Cacao Bar occupy the top floor balcony, hovering under a gorgeous chandelier. As mind-altering as one of MarieBelle's chocolate morsels taste, it is owner and chocolatier Maribel Lieberman and her nephew, Rodolfo, who truly warm the hearts of many, us included.

We visited Limelight on its opening day, seeking MarieBelle, a crowded and upbeat affair for sure. And even in the midst of the crowds and hungry customers, both Maribel and Rodolfo charmingly conversed and talked a little "shop" with us. Gracious, warm, and incredibly talented, Maribel Lieberman is a one-of-a-kind chocolatier.

Flatiron PROFESSOR PICKS
May we suggest our favorites?
• Mini Fin du Chocolat • Aztec Mocha Hot Chocolate
• Coeur de Guanaja 80% Dark Chocolate

MarieBelle
Purchases

Truffles & Bonbons:

Name/Description:

Rating: ☆☆☆☆☆

Name/Description:

Rating: ☆☆☆☆☆

Name/Description:

Rating: ☆☆☆☆☆

Name/Description:

Rating: ☆☆☆☆☆

Bars & Barks:

Name/Description:

Rating: ☆☆☆☆☆

Name/Description:

Rating: ☆☆☆☆☆

Name/Description:

Rating: ☆☆☆☆☆

Drinks & Others:

Name/Description:

Rating: ☆☆☆☆☆

Name/Description:

Rating: ☆☆☆☆☆

Flatiron COCOATASTIC TOUR

Notes:

Share your feedback with us @ professorchocolate.com

❹ L'atelier du chocolat
59 W 22nd Street
New York, NY 10011
212.414.2462
egchocolates.com

CHOCOLATIER:
Eric Girerd

CHOCOLATE USED:
· Valrhona 72% Dark Chocolate

History:
Master chocolatier Eric Girerd and wife Nam Hee opened L'atelier du chocolat in October of 2008. However new the sleek Flatiron shop may be, the master behind the chocolate earned his stripes over a career that has spanned close to four decades in the art of making pastry and chocolate.

Girerd started his pastry career at the three star Michelin-ranked Auberge du Pere Bise Talloire located in Paris. From the 1980s until 2002, Girerd racked up substantial frequent flyer miles as he dotted revered restaurants from New York City to Tokyo to Morocco to Seoul.

It was in 2002 that Girerd officially started L'atelier du chocolat out of Greenpoint, Brooklyn. Since then he has exclusively used Valrhona chocolate to create a variety of truffles that are now crafted in New

Jersey. The petite chocolate boutique packs a potent and exotic chocolate punch, using fresh and haute couture ingredients.

Experience:
Third generation chocolatier Eric Girerd blends bold and intoxicating flavors from Asia and France, making his store one of the more exclusive choco-gastronmic undertakings in New York. The slick and alcove-like L'atelier storefront can be easily passed by, so don't sneeze.
Take a deep breath and pause before entering L'atelier. Prepare to be immediately greeted by shopkeepers who are very proud of the delicate and sophisticated French-inspired product.

Knowledgeable and accommodating, the shopkeepers, one of whom is Girerd's wife, are always eager to assist in your pursuit of

HOURS:
Mon—Sat: 10am—7pm

SUBWAYS:
F, M to 23rd Street
N, R to 23rd Street

SHIPPING:
Orders placed by 1pm are shipped
the same day. Shipments are made
Monday through Thursday via UPS.

couture chocolate. Small as the store
may be, there are enough bonbons
in the shiny display case to keep one
busy for quite some time.

Though it's hard to go wrong
when choosing from the handsomely
displayed bonbons, try the intoxicating Jasmine Tea or the Ylang-Ylang.
One bite and this tiny sanctuary of
heavenly cocoa will seem like an ex-
panse of new flavor experiences.

Flatiron PROFESSOR PICKS
May we suggest our favorites?
• Oak-Smoked Salt Bonbons
• Wasabi Bonbons

L'atelier du chocolat
Purchases

Truffles & Bonbons:

Name/Description:

Rating: ☆☆☆☆☆

Name/Description:

Rating: ☆☆☆☆☆

Name/Description:

Rating: ☆☆☆☆☆

Name/Description:

Rating: ☆☆☆☆☆

Bars & Barks:

Name/Description:

Rating: ☆☆☆☆☆

Name/Description:

Rating: ☆☆☆☆☆

Name/Description:

Rating: ☆☆☆☆☆

Drinks & Others:

Name/Description:

Rating: ☆☆☆☆☆

Name/Description:

Rating: ☆☆☆☆☆

Flatiron COCOATASTIC TOUR

Notes:

5 FIKA espresso bar

407 Park Avenue South
New York, NY 10016
646.649.5133
fikanyc.com

CHOCOLATIER:
Håkan Mårtensson

CHOCOLATE USED:
· Barry Callebaut

History:

Swedish culture loves coffee. So much so that they are one of the world's leading consumers of coffee; and not just any old cup, really good coffee. Leave it to Lars Akerlund and David Johansson to transplant their beloved home country's zest for coffee to New York. They opened the FIKA espresso bar in 2006, specializing in Arabica beans flown in from a 100-year-old roaster in Sweden. Fika is a Swedish verb that literally translates to "take a coffee break accompanied by something toothsome and yummy." Enter FIKA Choklad.

One of Europe's best pastry chefs and chocolatiers, Håkan Mårtensson, was himself sourced from Sweden in 2008 to expand the FIKA menu beyond sweets and coffee. Mårtensson holds the gold medal in the 2008 food olympics for his mastery of decorative chocolate.

Drawing from fairy tales and a deep imagination, Mårtensson creates riveting chocolate sculptures with focused intensity.

Aside from chocolate sculptures, Mårtensson also handcrafts sumptuous truffles, bars and pralines of many different colors, shapes, and names can now be found in three different Manhattan locations. This shop, FIKA's second, opened in 2008, while the flagship store opened up in the Financial District in early 2010 (See chapter 1).

Experience:

Though FIKA is quickly expanding, with brand new digs at the southern tip of the island, the Flatiron shop is a bite-size excursion into Swedish life. Though coffee and pastries were the original draw for fans of FIKA, the addition of chocolatier Håkan Mårtensson registers FIKA as

HOURS:
Mon—Fri: 7am—7pm
Sat: 9am—6pm
Sun: 10am—4pm

SUBWAYS:
6 to 28th Street
N, R to 28th Street

ADDITIONAL INFO:
Catering services available.

h

a chocolate hot-spot.

Coffee at FIKA is not meant to be quaffed on the go, you are meant to sit, enjoy, and talk with friends with the serious cup of brew. Even more gratifying is to sample one of the dozen or so chocolates neatly displayed while you sip your new found love of drinking coffee- while sitting. How novel!

One of our favorite bonbons here is the Espresso, never too strong and never any "coffee" aftertaste.

Flatiron PROFESSOR PICKS
May we suggest our favorites?
• White Chocolate Hand-Rolled Truffles
• Signature Espresso

Flatiron COCOATASTIC TOUR

FIKA espresso bar
Purchases

Truffles & Bonbons:

Name/Description:

Rating: ☆☆☆☆☆

Name/Description:

Rating: ☆☆☆☆☆

Name/Description:

Rating: ☆☆☆☆☆

Name/Description:

Rating: ☆☆☆☆☆

Bars & Barks:

Name/Description:

Rating: ☆☆☆☆☆

Name/Description:

Rating: ☆☆☆☆☆

Name/Description:

Rating: ☆☆☆☆☆

Drinks & Others:

Name/Description:

Rating: ☆☆☆☆☆

Name/Description:

Rating: ☆☆☆☆☆

Flatiron COCOATASTIC TOUR

Notes:

Share your feedback with us @ professorchocolate.com

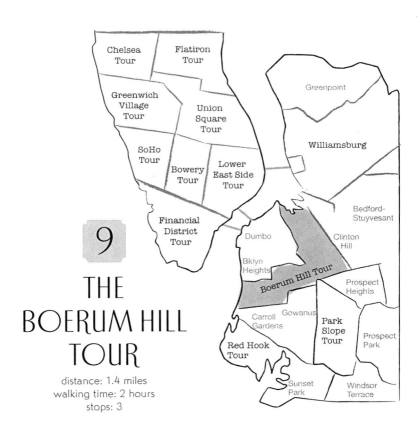

9

THE BOERUM HILL TOUR

distance: 1.4 miles
walking time: 2 hours
stops: 3

In the late 1880s wealthy merchants staked their claim in Brooklyn by building sumptuous brownstones. Today, "Brownstone Brooklyn" comprises a handful of charming and distinctive neighborhoods replete with a myriad of boutique shops. The local shops on Smith Street, Court Street, and the western portion of Atlantic Avenue, specialize in anything from cakes, cookies, fashion, vintage accessories, coffee, furniture, and, of course, chocolate. The quaint and picturesque neighborhoods remain on the short list of some of the most desirable places to live in New York City. The "Boerum Hill Tour" actually spans across three neighborhoods. It dips into Fort Greene to the north and Cobble Hill to the south.

Boerum Hill BROWNSTONE TOUR

Boerum Hill BROWNSTONE TOUR

1 Brooklyn Flea:
1 Hanson Place (corner of Hanson Place and Ashland Place)
Outdoors on Saturday and indoors on Sunday. Choose wisely. One of NYC's real architectural gems can be enjoyed while simultaneously shopping for vintage sunglasses and nibbling on chocolates from Nunu, LiddAbit, and Fine & Raw.

2 Nunu Chocolates:
529 Atlantic Avenue (between 3rd and 4th Avenues)
Pringle and Laird head up this tranquil joint on Atlantic Avenue. Beer is served with your choice of chocolate or you could opt for the beer-in-your-chocolate truffle. We like both.

3 The Chocolate Room:
269 Court Street (between Butler and Douglass Streets)
Mouth-watering chocolate cake, refreshing chocolate sorbet, and zippy chocolate shakes? Do you really need another reason to visit? Knipschildt bonbons and truffles are prominently displayed as well, in case you do.

White chocolate is typically made from cocoa butter, sugar, and milk products. The cocoa content is 0%.

Boerum Hill LOCAL STOPS

A Brooklyn Flea:
1 Hanson Place (corner of Hanson and Ashland Places)
One-stop shopping for all of your vintage goods and, dare we say, some of the best street-vendor food in the city, from chocolate to coffee to fish tacos. Outside on Saturdays, inside at Hanson Place on Sundays.

B Betty Bakery:
448 Atlantic Avenue (between Nevins and Bond Streets)
This cake shop sells its share of wedding cakes, but snacking will do just fine here, too. Usually on display are decorative cookies and pastries created by some very talented pastry chefs. Certainly one of the better bakeries for the vintage favorite, Red Velvet Cake.

C One Girl Cookies:
68 Dean Street (between Smith Street and Boerum Place)
Upon seeing the "One Girl Cookie" sign, we immediately bolted to the door and busted in with childlike giddiness. Completely dedicated to the art of making bite-size cookies, this shop can't be missed. Seating available if you're one for savoring the little morsels.

Boerum Hill BROWNSTONE TOUR

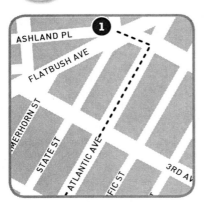

❶ Brooklyn Flea

1 Hanson Place
Brooklyn ,NY 11217
718.783.2900
brooklynflea.com

CHOCOLATIERS:
Nunu (Andy Laird and Justine Pringle)
Fine and Raw (Daniel Sklaar)
LiddAbit (Liz Gutman and Jen King)

History:

This Brooklyn flea market takes place on weekends at two locations. Indoors it's at 1 Hanson Place, a.k.a. the Williamsburgh Savings Bank. The Bishop Loughlin High School in Fort Greene houses the all-day event on Saturdays. It is, however, the Williamsburgh Savings Bank that is architecturally captivating and worthy of a visit with or without the draw of vintage goods and chocolate.

The first few stories were built in 1875, only to see a complete makeover in 1927 by its new owner, the Williamsburgh Savings Bank. Hotshot architects at the time built the 512-foot skyscraper in three years. It is still one of the tallest clock towers in the world. Magic Johnson, who has renovated the building with luxury condos, presently owns it.

Even more spectacular than its exterior, is the 63-foot vaulted ceiling

that was once over the heartbeat of Brooklyn banking. The glorious marble structure is now home to Brooklyn Flea on Sundays, and has one of the more breathtaking interiors in all of NYC.

Experience:

Though Brooklyn Flea is not a chocolate destination itself, there are a few chocolate/sweets vendors, all worth your time. If you've not been to Brooklyn Flea, you are doing yourself a great injustice, for this is not your mother's flea market. Brooklyn Flea is replete with everything from vintage furniture and clothes to renovated bikes to killer shades to trendy onesies for your baby.

Clothes and accessories not jiving with you? The food certainly will. From Vietnamese sandwiches, prosciutto and ricotta cheese on a soft baguette, and crunchy tacos; to cookies, cupcakes, and of course, chocolate you'll be

HOURS:
Sunday: 10am—5pm

SUBWAYS:
C to Lafayette Avenue
2, 3 to Bergen Street
2, 3, 4, 5, B, Q to Atlantic Avenue
N, R, D to Pacific Street

ADDITIONAL INFO:
On Saturday, the Brooklyn Flea
operates outdoors at 176 Lafayette
Avenue in nearby Fort Greene,
Brooklyn

fully satisfied. Three vendors now sell chocolate or chocolate-inspired goods at the Flea, all very different from one another: Nunu (profiled separately on this tour), Fine & Raw, and LiddAbit.

Fine & Raw is dedicated to the fine art of creating completely raw chocolate. All of the confections, created by a former New York financier, are crafted using low-heat technology. This allows the "raw" state of chocolate to remain intact, thus preserving the liveliness and nutrients naturally found in chocolate. One of our favorites is the creamy Crystal and Sea Salt bar.

Also making waves at Brooklyn Flea, and other specialty food shops,

are the addictive candy and chocolates made by LiddAbit. The two young women, Liz Gutman and Jen King, met each other at the French Culinary Institute and instantly formed a bond. The two realized they had a passion for preparing sweets that included a philosophy of using ingredients that only "local, artisanal, and seasonal." No stores as of yet, so visit the smiling duo at Brooklyn Flea. Try the Snacker bar, a cousin of You-Know-Who but even more scrumptious.

Boerum Hill PROFESSOR PICKS

May we suggest our favorites?
• The Snacker by LiddABit
• Nunu hand-dipped soft caramels
• Cacao and Coconut Chunky Bonbons by Fine and Raw

Boerum Hill BROWNSTONE TOUR

Brooklyn Flea
Purchases

Truffles & Bonbons:

Name/Description:

_____ Rating: ☆☆☆☆☆

Name/Description:

_____ Rating: ☆☆☆☆☆

Name/Description:

_____ Rating: ☆☆☆☆☆

Name/Description:

_____ Rating: ☆☆☆☆☆

Bars & Barks:

Name/Description:

_____ Rating: ☆☆☆☆☆

Name/Description:

_____ Rating: ☆☆☆☆☆

Name/Description:

_____ Rating: ☆☆☆☆☆

Drinks & Others:

Name/Description:

_____ Rating: ☆☆☆☆☆

Name/Description:

_____ Rating: ☆☆☆☆☆

Notes:

Share your feedback with us @ professorchocolate.com

❷ Nunu Chocolates

529 Atlantic Avenue
Brooklyn, NY 11217
917.776.7102
nunuchocolates.com

CHOCOLATIER:
Andy Laird and Justine Pringle

CHOCOLATE USED:
Single-origin cacao beans derived from
a Trintario and Criollo hybrid from a
family run farm in eastern Columbia.

History:

A few years back Andy Laird was performing live with his band while his girlfriend, Justine Pringle, was cooking up ideas on what else to sell at the band's merchandise table. There were the obligatory hats and T-shirts, but something more was calling Pringle. A special satisfaction came in the form of selling homemade chocolates at Laird's gigs.

Inspired so much by the heartfilled goodness that chocolate seems to evoke, the couple set aside their day jobs and leapfrogged their way into the world of chocolate. In 2008, the now-married couple opened their flagship store on Atlantic Avenue in Boerum Hill, Brooklyn. Their shop was lovingly named Nunu, the affectionate moniker given to children in South Africa, Pringle's native country. And if you're keeping count, Laird and Pringle are one of three husband-

wife chocolate teams in Brooklyn.

Before her chocolatier days, Pringle had started a career in environmental waste management, but quickly discovered that the science of making chocolate was much more interesting...we agree! Her formal training in waste management has not fully escaped her however. Pringle only sources her cacao beans from a family-run plantation that practices sustainable farming. The world is certainly a better place with people like Laird and Pringle.

Experience:

The husband-wife team of Andy Laird and Justine Pringle taste-tested many a chocolate bar before opening Nunu. Their goal was to discover the types of chocolate that evoked the most pleasure and emotion, and friends and family gladly helped in this endeavor. Pringle was able to

Boerum Hill BROWNSTONE TOUR

HOURS:
Open daily: 7am—9pm

SUBWAYS:
2, 3, 4, 5, B, Q to Atlantic Avenue
N, R, D to Pacific Street
G to Fulton Street

SHIPPING:
Via FedEx

pinpoint and then stamp her own brand of chocolate morsels, creating a niche within the growing market for chocolate.

Nunu creates a full array of truffles, but some of our favorites include those with boozy overtones. The Absinthe Delight is as unique and exciting as truffles go, not to mention strangely addictive. For spicy alcohol lovers, Nunu makes a mean Mezcal Chili Truffle, zippy and fresh. Though these truffles can be found at various specialty shops, the safest bet is to visit the only Nunu storefront, on Atlantic Avenue in Brooklyn.

Nunu had been open only one year when the couple decided to renovate the joint in the fall of 2009. Comfy furniture and tables were placed near the large bay window, and they added a full-blown coffee and espresso bar. In addition, three finely crafted American beers are usually on tap, to accompany a slew of bottled beer, making Nunu a destination replete with chocolate, beer, and coffee. There can be no excuses! Cross the river and visit one of Brooklyn's finest.

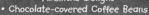

Boerum Hill PROFESSOR PICKS
May we suggest our favorites?
• Absinthe Delight
• Chocolate-covered Coffee Beans

Nunu Chocolates
Purchases

Truffles & Bonbons:

Name/Description:

Rating: ☆☆☆☆☆

Name/Description:

Rating: ☆☆☆☆☆

Name/Description:

Rating: ☆☆☆☆☆

Name/Description:

Rating: ☆☆☆☆☆

Bars & Barks:

Name/Description:

Rating: ☆☆☆☆☆

Name/Description:

Rating: ☆☆☆☆☆

Name/Description:

Rating: ☆☆☆☆☆

Drinks & Others:

Name/Description:

Rating: ☆☆☆☆☆

Name/Description:

Rating: ☆☆☆☆☆

Notes:

Share your feedback with us @ professorchocolate.com

❸ The Chocolate Room

269 Court Street
Brooklyn, NY 11231
718.246.2600
thechocolateroombrooklyn.com

CHOCOLATIER:
Fritz Knipschildt and Made'casse

CHOCOLATE USED:
· Ezaka Cocoa Cooperative
· Valrhona
· Michel Cluizel
· Belcolade

History:

Thanks in large part to people like Jon Payson and Naomi Josepher, the husband-wife team who own and run the Chocolate Room, Brooklyn neighborhoods just happen to be a better place to live and play. Not only does the couple and their staff serve-up a luscious, chocolate-themed dessert menu, they do so with a genuine smile.

As the story goes, Jon and Naomi met a few years back while waiting tables, each trying to jump-start their fledgling careers in the arts— Jon a drummer, Naomi a Modern dancer. Over the course of a few years, one thing led to another, and the two began to share a vision of bringing a great chocolate house to Brooklyn. After being inspired by an article on how the chocolate niche was fast-becoming the "new coffee," the seed was sewn to open a unique chocolate café in Brooklyn.

In 2003 they helped to revitalize the 5th Avenue section of Park Slope by opening up the original Chocolate Room. A few years later, Jon and Naomi decided to expand their chocolate refuge onto Court Street in the Cobble Hill section of Brooklyn. The area was already brimming with charm, a perfect locale for a new Chocolate Room. Maybe one of the smartest moves was to locate the Court Street location next to the Cobble Hill Cinemas movie theater. We personally make trips to that movie theater simply because the Chocolate Room is right next door!

Experience:

Stepping into either one of the Chocolate Room venues, one cannot help but notice two striking features: the smiling staff and the cozy decor. The lit candles, exposed brick, and

HOURS:
Sun—Thurs: Noon—11pm
Fri and Sat: Noon—Midnight

SUBWAYS:
F, G to Bergen Street

SHIPPING:
Preferred shipping method is
next-day air

ADDITIONAL INFO:
*To learn more about Project Ezaka,
inquire at The Chocolate Room or write
to info@madecasse.com.*

white tin ceilings add an element of romance, especially if you stop by after dinner. Truffle and bonbon lovers will immediately be pulled to the prominently stationed display case, courtesy of Fritz Knipschildt. (For more on Knipschildt, see profile in chapter 5).

Piquant morsels of chocolate can be found in many a chocolate boutique, but the Chocolate Room's real specialty is revealed in their chocolate-centered dessert menu. Chocolate floats, several different kinds of hot chocolate, the decadent chocolate layer cake, butterscotch pudding and even wine and alcohol pairings can be found here.

Though the truffles are not made on-site, the rest of the des-

serts and ingredients for the drinks are all "homemade," lovingly created by the close-knit staff.

Boerum Hill **BROWNSTONE TOUR**

The Chocolate Room
Purchases

Truffles & Bonbons:

Name/Description:

Rating: ☆☆☆☆☆

Name/Description:

Rating: ☆☆☆☆☆

Name/Description:

Rating: ☆☆☆☆☆

Name/Description:

Rating: ☆☆☆☆☆

Bars & Barks:

Name/Description:

Rating: ☆☆☆☆☆

Name/Description:

Rating: ☆☆☆☆☆

Name/Description:

Rating: ☆☆☆☆☆

Drinks & Others:

Name/Description:

Rating: ☆☆☆☆☆

Name/Description:

Rating: ☆☆☆☆☆

Notes:

Share your feedback with us @ professorchocolate.com

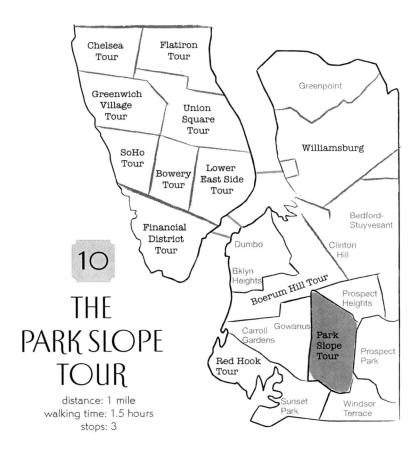

10

THE PARK SLOPE TOUR

distance: 1 mile
walking time: 1.5 hours
stops: 3

Bound by Prospect Park to the east and Flatbush Avenue to the north, there are very few places in New York City that are more desirable to reside in than Park Slope, Brooklyn. In fact, The American Planning Association rated Park Slope as "one of the greatest neighborhoods in America" in 2007. New York magazine echoed these sentiments in June of 2010, claiming that Park Slope was New York's best overall neighborhood. Its proximity to Prospect Park, multiple subway lines, child-friendly activities, and the ubiquitous restaurant and bar scene all contribute to the highly attractive nature of 'the Slope.'

Park Slope STROLLER TOUR

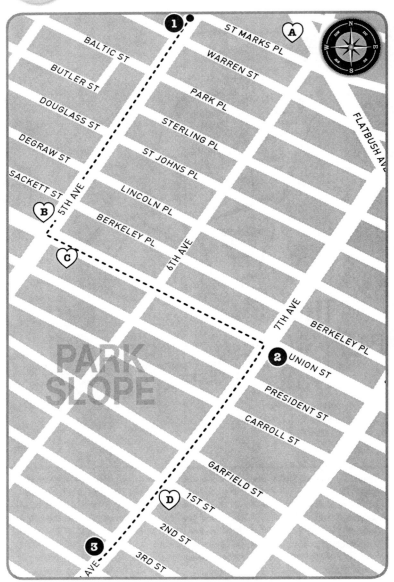

Park Slope STROLLER TOUR

1 **The Chocolate Room:**
86 Fifth Avenue (between St. Marks Place and Warren Street)
The fun-loving husband-and-wife team of Jon and Naomi satisfies every possible chocolate urge at their original location on 5th Avenue. Knipschildt Chocolates available in spades.

2 **Blue Apron Foods:**
814 Union Street (near the corner of 7th Avenue)
Though this store does not specialize in chocolate, the fine array of exotic chocolate bars and a varied display of truffles will keep you coming back to this neighborhood favorite.

3 **Cocoa Bar:**
228 7th Avenue (between 3rd and 4th Streets)
Bring your laptop to this cafe/chocolate bar. Wine is paired with your truffles and other fine desserts. Ample seating and a cozy spot for that after-dinner urge for sweets.

> 100g of chocolate can supply 50% of a person's dietary requirement of copper, which is important for energy production and nerve health.

Park Slope LOCAL STOPS

A **Brooklyn Larder:** *228 Flatbush Avenue (between St. Marks Place and Bergen Street)*
A festivity of food. Slow food, that is. Premium cheeses and meats that make us salivate just thinking about the place. Artisanal ice cream, olive oils, teas, and chocolates will surely convince you to linger a while. The heirloom pork sausage is reason enough for a visit.

B **Bierkraft:** *191 Fifth Avenue (between Berkeley and Union Streets)*
Beer! A tantalizing array of domestic and international beers greets you as soon as you walk in. Be sure to make your way to the back where there's usually some kind of secret draft being masterfully crafted. Don't forget your growler! Chocolate and cheese also available along with ample seating.

C **Union Hall:** *702 Union Street (near the corner of Union Street and 5th Avenue)*
A neighborhood favorite with a serious collection of beers. Space is plentiful even though it houses a bocce ball court. A basement area sometimes plays host to quirky events. We once attended an evening devoted to essays and pictures on "weird science." Need we say more?

D **Sweet Melissa Patisserie:** *175 7th Avenue (between 1st and 2nd Streets)*
French-style coffee, pastries, and bread are for the taking here. Elegant and tiny, the shop boasts a few places to sit and now, one of our favorites, homemade ice cream.

Park Slope STROLLER TOUR

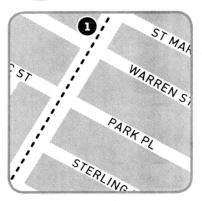

❶ The Chocolate Room

86 5th Avenue
Brooklyn, NY 11217
718.783.2900
thechocolateroombrooklyn.com

CHOCOLATIER:
Fritz Knipschildt and Made'casse

CHOCOLATE USED:
· Ezaka Cocoa Cooperative
· Valrhona
· Michel Cluizel
· Belcolade

History:

Not so long ago the 5th Avenue slice of Park Slope, Brooklyn was hardly the magnet area of lively restaurants, bars, and restored brownstones that it is today. Blown-out buildings and squalor were present in lieu of the lively scene of today. By 2005, 5th Avenue was fully emerged in a renaissance thanks in large part to people like Jon Payson and Naomi Josepher, the husband-wife team who own and run The Chocolate Room.

Jon and Naomi met a few years back while waiting tables, each trying to jumpstart their fledgling careers in the arts. Jon, a drummer; Naomi, a modern dancer. Over the course of a few years, one thing led to another, and the two began to share a vision of being part of the much talked about "5th Avenue renaissance." After being inspired by an article on how the chocolate niche

was fast-becoming the "new coffee," the seed was sewn to open a chocolate boutique in Brooklyn.

The married couple bought the space in 2003 and officially opened the doors on Valentine's Day, 2005. There has been no looking back as the two opened up another shop on Court Street in Cobble Hill, not far form Park Slope (see previous chapter).

Experience:

Stepping into either one of The Chocolate Room venues, one cannot help but notice two striking features: the smiling staff and the cozy decor. The lit candles, exposed brick, and white tin ceilings add an element of romance, especially if you stop by after dinner. Truffle and bonbon lovers will immediately be pulled to the prominently stationed display case, courtesy of Fritz Knipschildt. (For

Park Slope STROLLER TOUR

HOURS:
Sun—Thurs: Noon—11pm
Fri and Sat: Noon—Midnight

SUBWAYS:
2, 3 to Bergen Street
2, 3, 4, 5, B, Q to Atlantic Avenue
N, R, D to Pacific Street

SHIPPING:
Preferred shipping method is
next-day air

ADDITIONAL INFO:
*To learn about Project Ezaka, inquire at
The Chocolate Room or write to
info@madecasse.com*

more on Knipschildt, see profile in the Union Square Tour Section.)

Piquant morsels of chocolate can be found in many a chocolate boutique, but The Chocolate Room's real specialty is truly revealed on their chocolate-centered dessert menu. Chocolate floats, several different kinds of hot chocolate, the decadent chocolate layer cake, butterscotch pudding and even wine and alcohol pairings can be found here. On a recent visit, we enjoyed homemade ice cream shakes, fresh, with none of that residual sensation of feeling bloated.

Though the chocolates are not

made on-site, the rest of the desserts and ingredients for the dessert drinks are all "homemade," lovingly created by the close-knit staff.

The Chocolate Room
Purchases

Truffles & Bonbons:

Name/Description:_____

_____ Rating: ☆☆☆☆☆

Name/Description:_____

_____ Rating: ☆☆☆☆☆

Name/Description:_____

_____ Rating: ☆☆☆☆☆

Name/Description:_____

_____ Rating: ☆☆☆☆☆

Bars & Barks:

Name/Description:_____

_____ Rating: ☆☆☆☆☆

Name/Description:_____

_____ Rating: ☆☆☆☆☆

Name/Description:_____

_____ Rating: ☆☆☆☆☆

Drinks & Others:

Name/Description:_____

_____ Rating: ☆☆☆☆☆

Name/Description:_____

_____ Rating: ☆☆☆☆☆

Park Slope **STROLLER TOUR**

Notes:

_____
_____
_____
_____
_____
_____
_____
_____
_____
_____
_____

Share your feedback with us @ professorchocolate.com

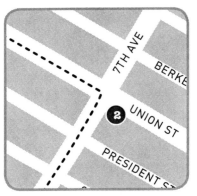

Park Slope STROLLER TOUR

② Blue Apron Foods
814 Union Street
Brooklyn, NY 11215
718.230.3180

OWNER:
Al Palmer

CHOCOLATE:
Blue Apron carries a variety of local and imported artisanal chocolates.

History:
There may not be a more apropos niche in New York than Park Slope, Brooklyn, to open up a shop devoted to slow-food philosophy. Teeming with restaurants that use locally sourced and artisanal ingredients, Park Slope has become a mecca for the slow-food obsessed.

Proudly serving the foodie denizens of the area since 2002, Blue Apron maintains a loyal customer base that only seems to be growing. The star of the show is hands-on owner Al Palmer, a veritable encyclopedia of New York food for the last 20 years. No Johnny-come-lately here, Palmer has devoted his life to the slow-food movement, evidenced by the cornucopia of fine products lining the shelves at Blue Apron.

The store is chock-full of locally sourced cheeses, olive oils, meats, prepared meals, ice cream, and choc-

olate. So enticing are these items that Blue Apron received the "Snail of Approval" by Slow Food NYC, an organization that prides itself on finding the city's best foraging spots (see slow-foodnyc.org for a complete listing).

Experience:
Park Slope's 5th and 7th Avenues are lined with an inordinate amount of specialty stores and restaurants, most of them privately owned. Blue Apron Foods fits the bill just as elegantly as any other store and may very well be one of the friendliest.

Al, the owner of Blue Apron Foods, is not a chocolatier but boasts a bounty of different kinds of chocolate bars and bonbons. The chocolate bars are as diverse in flavor as their makers are in personality and origin, though many bars are locally sourced. The bonbon collection is supplied by Nunu, which appears in

HOURS:
Tue—Fri: 10am—7:30pm
Sat: 9am—7pm
Sun: 10am—6pm

SUBWAYS:
2, 3 to Grand Army Plaza
B, Q to 7th Avenue
R to Union Street

the Boerum Hill Brownstone Tour. At one time there had also been some truffles from Vintage Chocolates in New Jersey.

Cheeses, prosciutto, oils, and other fine edible goods can also be discovered here. The shop is small, and the staff friendly and helpful. Quite possibly the finest treat is to watch Al interact with his loyal customer base. He is an owner who cares about the shop, his customers, and the slow-food scene that seems to be bursting at the seams. Simply delicious.

Park Slope PROFESSOR PICKS
May we suggest our favorites?
• LiddAbit King Bars
• Nunu Salted Caramels

Park Slope STROLLER TOUR

Blue Apron Foods
Purchases

Truffles & Bonbons:

Name/Description:

Rating: ☆☆☆☆☆

Name/Description:

Rating: ☆☆☆☆☆

Name/Description:

Rating: ☆☆☆☆☆

Name/Description:

Rating: ☆☆☆☆☆

Bars & Barks:

Name/Description:

Rating: ☆☆☆☆☆

Name/Description:

Rating: ☆☆☆☆☆

Name/Description:

Rating: ☆☆☆☆☆

Drinks & Others:

Name/Description:

Rating: ☆☆☆☆☆

Name/Description:

Rating: ☆☆☆☆☆

Park Slope STROLLER TOUR

Notes:

Share your feedback with us @ professorchocolate.com

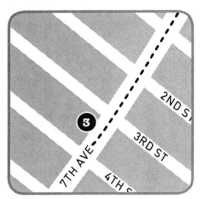

❸ Cocoa Bar

228 7th Avenue
Brooklyn, NY 11215
718.499.4080
cocoabarnyc.com

OWNERS:
Liat Cohen and Yaniv Reeis

CHOCOLATIER:
Michel Cluizel bonbons are imported
from France

History:

Cocoa Bar has two New York City locations, the original is located in Park Slope, Brooklyn and the second is ensconced in the hip n' trendy Lower East Side (see chapter 4). Owned by the husband-wife team of Liat Cohen and Yaniv Reeis, Cocoa Bar has become a neighborhood fixture in both locations.

2005 marked the beginning for the Cocoa Bar, but it didn't come without some major risks for the spousal team. One of which is the fact that Park Slope had been, and still is, laden with popular cafés such as Ozzie's, the Tea Lounge, and Starbucks. In the past few years more cafés have joined the ranks of Park Slope niches, usually enjoying the patronage of the of high-standard obsessed locals.

With that being said, the combining triage of bakery/coffee shop/wine house is eclectic enough to

be unique, but also popular enough to stay in business. At some point, the Cocoa Bar in both locations may have used Leonidas chocolates, from Belgium. More recently though, we were informed that Michel Cluizel Chocolates, sent express from Danville, France, are awaiting your consumption.

Experience:

The Park Slope location is as laid back a chocolate shop cum coffee house as one can get. Comfy furniture and brown-hued tones make the Cocoa Bar perfect for the studious on a weekday afternoon or the romantic couple looking for an after-dinner dessert snack. Paintings by local artist adorn the walls creating a meditative and tranquil atmosphere. The Cocoa Bar can at times feel like an arty coffee shop, but one that sells delicious chocolate and other goodies.

Park Slope STROLLER TOUR

HOURS:
Mon—Thurs: 7am—12am
Fri: 7am—1am
Sat: 8am—1am
Sun: 8am—12am

SUBWAYS:
F, G to Bergen Street

The chocolate pastries are homemade and are certainly worth sampling. However, with the myriad of boutiques listed in this book, the Cocoa Bar has a certain unique twist when it comes to the sit-down experience. Though it may be called the Cocoa Bar, it is certainly more than that, and certainly worth your time to experience some of the chocolate infused desserts.

The menu is extensive, and very fun, especially if you like to pair your wine with chocolate. The knowledge-able staff and explanatory menu can make this destination a dining experience unto itself. The scrumptious Flourless Chocolate cake is a slice of heaven sipped with one of their red wine selections. Check out their live jazz shows on steamy summer nights for a cool as a cat experience.

Park Slope PROFESSOR PICKS
May we suggest our favorites?
• Flourless Chocolate Cake
• Cinnamon Hot Chocolate

Park Slope STROLLER TOUR

Cocoa Bar Purchases

Truffles & Bonbons:

Name/Description:

Rating: ☆☆☆☆☆

Name/Description:

Rating: ☆☆☆☆☆

Name/Description:

Rating: ☆☆☆☆☆

Name/Description:

Rating: ☆☆☆☆☆

Bars & Barks:

Name/Description:

Rating: ☆☆☆☆☆

Name/Description:

Rating: ☆☆☆☆☆

Name/Description:

Rating: ☆☆☆☆☆

Drinks & Others:

Name/Description:

Rating: ☆☆☆☆☆

Name/Description:

Rating: ☆☆☆☆☆

Park Slope **STROLLER TOUR**

Notes:

_____
_____
_____
_____
_____
_____
_____
_____
_____
_____
_____
_____

Share your feedback with us @ professorchocolate.com

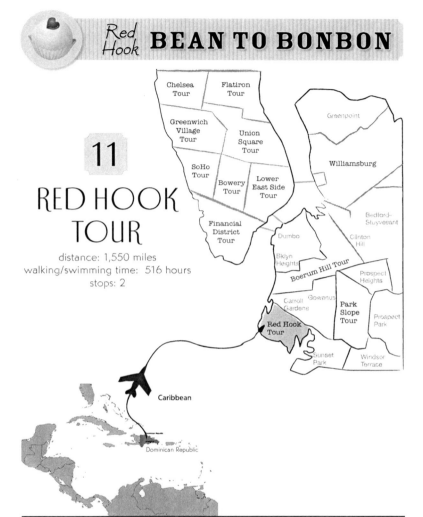

11

RED HOOK
TOUR

distance: 1,550 miles
walking/swimming time: 516 hours
stops: 2

Chelsea Tour

Flatiron Tour

Greenwich Village Tour

Union Square Tour

Greenpoint

SoHo Tour

Bowery Tour

Lower East Side Tour

Williamsburg

Financial District Tour

Dumbo

Bklyn Heights

Clinton Hill

Bedford-Stuyvesant

Boerum Hill Tour

Prospect Heights

Carroll Gardens

Gowanus

Park Slope Tour

Prospect Park

Red Hook Tour

Sunset Park

Windsor Terrace

Caribbean

Dominican Republic

Located in the northeastern corner of Brooklyn, lies what many New Yorkers would call a quaint and quiet town. Red Hook, named Roode Hoek by the Dutch in the 17th century, is the site of the first European child born in the New World. In more recent times, Red Hook had been the site for busy docks and warehouses, many of which are now converted to everything from Ikea to soap and flower shops. The later part of the 20th century brought urban blight upon many doorsteps, but much has changed in the last ten years. A renaissance of sorts has struck the once troubled town, bringing with it clothing boutiques, vintage wares, restaurants, bars, flower shops, and, of course, Ikea. Follow Van Brunt Street, which runs from the docks to the edge of Carroll Gardens, Cobble Hill and downtown Brooklyn, for the bulk of shopping and eating in Red Hook. Many gems, however, can be discovered by walking the side streets.

Red Hook BEAN TO BONBON

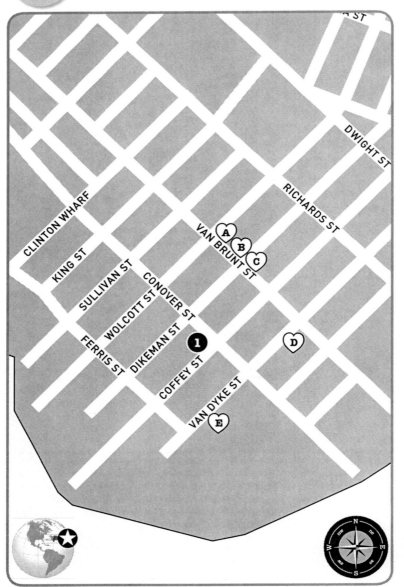

CLINTON WHARF

DWIGHT ST

RICHARDS ST

VAN BRUNT ST

KING ST

SULLIVAN ST

CONOVER ST

WOLCOTT ST

FERRIS ST

DIKEMAN ST

COFFEY ST

VAN DYKE ST

A B C

D

E

1

BEAN TO BONBON

❶ Cacao Prieto (at Botanica):

220 Conover Street (@ Coffey Street)

Stellar cocktails and sinister chocolate make a splash at this classy Red Hook joint. Need we give you another reason to visit? If you insist ... Owner/pioneer Daniel Preston has his cacao beans shipped from his family-run plantations in the Dominica. Upon arrival, the beans are placed in the talented hands of Damion Badalementi, a masterful chocolatier trained in Spain. The soft lighting, vintage bar, and open-air atmosphere do wonders for the soul. Call ahead for hours, they may be closed during the winter months.

✪ Dominican Republic:

Prieto Family Plantation (San Pedro de Macoris)

The Dominican Republic is the second largest Caribbean nation next to Cuba. The DR occupies close to 50,000 square miles on the island of Hispaniola, which it shares with the nation of Haiti. The DR is one of the top producers of fair-trade, organic cacao.

Red Hook LOCAL STOPS

Ⓐ Hope and Anchor:
347 Van Brunt Street (@ Wolcott Street)
Serving hearty diner food, along with a zippy cocktail list, Hope and Anchor never disappoints. Worth the visit for a meaty burger after a night of getting totally blotto. Don't miss karaoke Thursday through Saturday nights!

Ⓑ Baked:
359 Van Brunt Street (@ Dikeman Street)
Best known for their brownies and cupcakes...Renato Poliafito and Matt Lewis bring together the perfect combination of fresh design and comforting, American sweets. This place has gotten the attention of Oprah, Bobby Flay, Martha Stewart and of course, Professor Chocolate!

Ⓒ Fort Defiance:
365 Van Brunt Street (@ Dikeman Street)
A simple menu with local ingredients draws many crowds. The snazzy brunch menu and reasonably priced, yet strong, cocktails are also a reason to swing by.

Ⓓ Saipua:
147 Van Dyke Street (near Van Brunt Street in a converted garage/warehouse)
Besides a love of chocolate, we also have an addiction to handmade soap. Saipua helps feed these addictions with a melange of fragrances.

Ⓔ Steve's Key Lime Pie
204 Van Dyke Street (along the water)
Slightly off the beaten path—keep following the painted wooden signs, and you will soon be led to the ecstasy that is Steve's Key Lime Pie.

Red Hook **BEAN TO BONBON**

❶ Cacao Prieto (at Botanica)

220 Conover Street
Brooklyn, NY 11231
718.797.2297
cacaoprieto.com

CHOCOLATIER:
Damion Badalementi

CHOCOLATE USED:
Chocolate is produced on-site using cacao beans from the Prieto Family Plantation in the Dominican Republic.

History:

As of the publication date of this book, Botanica had opened for business, but the soon-to-be chocolate factory was still in the beginning phases of development. The history of Botanica may be short, but one of its owners, Daniel Preston, and head chocolatier, Damion Badalementi, have created a destination with much character and soul.

Preston is constantly on the move, and constantly trying to improve the way things work. He is the owner of over 100 patents and retired in his 20's, if you will, after selling a glass-blowing company that he started in his late teens. With some time on his hands, he took up the hobby of sky-diving, broke his neck on a awkward fall (through no fault of his own), and invested his energetic mind into improving the safety and overall quality of parachutes. It wasn't long before

Preston gave birth to the idea of satellite guided parachutes. Yup, he sold this business as well.

It was then that a friend approached him about opening a bar in Red Hook. With cutting edge technology and low atmospheric pressure, this bar, unlike any other (anywhere) would distill its own liquor from the fruit of the cacao tree. They would attempt to craft spirits with vivid flavors that get lost with more conventional methods of distillation.

Not only will Botanica be distilling its very own spirits in the brick factory next door, but they will be processing the cacao beans from handpicked plantations in Dominica. With the help of cutting-edge winnowers and other bean-to-chocolate machines, some of which Preston has designed and built with his own two hands, Botanica will also be making and selling its very own chocolate. In a somewhat complicated

Red Hook BEAN TO BONBON

HOURS:
Please call ahead, hours are seasonal.

TRANSPORTATION:
The Professors prefer to either drive or take the Water Taxi from Pier 11 in Manhattan.

procedure, every ounce of the cacao bean will be used not only to create bonbons onsite, but also as the raw ingredients for the range of spirits that they will be distilling. Preston and Co are literally revolutionizing two fields at once.

Walk anywhere in New York and buzzwords like local, fresh, raw, and homemade hum like busy bees. Botanica is directly in tune with this and then some. By the end of 2010, Botanica will also have its very own greenhouse, growing veggies and fruit that will be sold and/or used in the homemade spirits.

Experience:

Red Hook, Brooklyn is full of simple pleasures. As a getaway 'hood for New Yorkers looking for a tad bit of solace, some bike it to the town on weekend jaunts. Ikea and Fairway of course attract the masses, but for a more subtle experience, visiting the actual neighborhood gives one the feeling that despite the unobstructed view of the Statue of Liberty, Manhattan is a faraway and distant place.

Van Brunt Street is the main drag, lined with some of our favorite places to visit in the city. Steve's Key Lime Pie, delicate flowers and soaps at Saipua, stellar cocktails and food at Fort Defiance, scrumptious brownies and coffee at Baked, and of course a classy restaurant for foodies, the Good Fork. There's more too, but you get the idea.

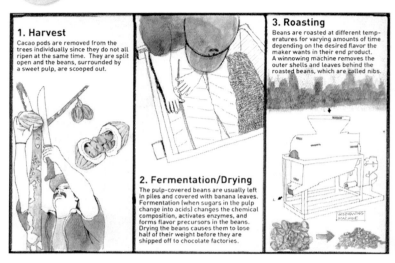

1. Harvest

Cacao pods are removed from the trees individually since they do not all ripen at the same time. They are split open and the beans, surrounded by a sweet pulp, are scooped out.

2. Fermentation/Drying

The pulp-covered beans are usually left in piles and covered with banana leaves. Fermentation (when sugars in the pulp change into acids) changes the chemical composition, activates enzymes, and forms flavor precursors in the beans. Drying the beans causes them to lose half of their weight before they are shipped off to chocolate factories.

3. Roasting

Beans are roasted at different temperatures for varying amounts of time depending on the desired flavor the maker wants in their end product. A winnowing machine removes the outer shells and leaves behind the roasted beans, which are called nibs.

Many of the neighborhoods we've profiled are enveloped by these types of shops, but Red Hook may just the most unique, a place that almost seems sleepy, lined with on-again, off-again cobble-stoned streets and converted warehouses that now hold plants, works of art, or, more pertinent to this book—chocolate.

On the corner of Conover and Coffey Streets sits Botanica, which at first glance, looks like a bar, but happens to be much more than that. The cocktails are laboriously concocted (some of the ingredients are even house-made) but it was the aroma of chocolate that attracted us to Botanica.

Daniel Preston and his girlfriend, Natalia, are warm and welcoming, with a visionary penchant for creativity and design. They have lovingly crafted the one room bar with an eye toward the 19th century. Vintage-style wooden tables and chairs line the shop, along with an attractive bar that captures one's attention

from the street. Both Daniel and Natalia have helped design a place that takes one back in time. We couldn't help but feel that we had been transported out of New York and onto a plantation living room with tall windows and a cool breeze. Botanica, much like Red Hook, is simply magical in that way.

Even more magical are the bonbons crafted by head chocolatier, Damion Badalementi. Talented and energetic, Badalementi is extremely passionate about making good chocolate. On a recent visit, he happily served some samples of his handcrafted bonbons, a transformative-like experience, one that every chocolate lover should experience. A self-described perfectionist, Badalementi is constantly tinkering with ingredients and techniques to create scintillating chocolate. By our measure, he lives up to the highest standards.

One of the chocolates we tried was the coconut bonbon which was so

4. Grinding
Milling, or grinding, the nibs, turns them into a thick liquid. Essentially, cocoa solids floating in cocoa butter. This is called chocolate liquor (even though it contains no alcohol).

5. Conching
Sugar and other ingredients can now be added to the liquor in preparation of conching. Machines called conches have heavy rollers which knead the chocolate for up to a week, giving it a smooth consistency.

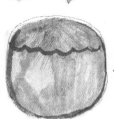

6. Tempering
The chocolate is now ready for tempering, which involves heating and cooling the chocolate. This affects the crystallization of the molecules as the chocolate sets in the bar or bonbon mold; and determines the appearance and consistency of the chocolate as it melts in your mouth!

authentically and naturally "coconut" that we felt as if we had been zipped off to some tropical island with crystal blue waters and sandy white beaches. We nearly had to be pinched. Next up was the Italian Biscotti bonbon. The first bite was so intense that for a moment we thought we were having dessert at a Tuscan Villa. Only a bona fide bonbon made with the utmost care and ingredients can capture one's imagination so fervently.

All of the bonbons, artfully crafted by Badalementi were vibrant and fresh, taking our conscious minds deep into the recesses of our imaginations. As unbelievable as it may be, Red Hook, Botanica, and the bonbons are the ingredients for a mind-altering and transformative experi-

ence. This is a lesson in chocolate that is well worth the trip.

Red Hook **PROFESSOR PICKS**
May we suggest our favorites?
• Coconut Ganache Bonbons
• Dominican Rum Ganache Bonbons

BEAN TO BONBON

Cacao Prieto
Purchases

Truffles & Bonbons:

Name/Description: _____

_____ Rating: ☆☆☆☆☆

Name/Description: _____

_____ Rating: ☆☆☆☆☆

Name/Description: _____

_____ Rating: ☆☆☆☆☆

Name/Description: _____

_____ Rating: ☆☆☆☆☆

Bars & Barks:

Name/Description: _____

_____ Rating: ☆☆☆☆☆

Name/Description: _____

_____ Rating: ☆☆☆☆☆

Name/Description: _____

_____ Rating: ☆☆☆☆☆

Drinks & Others:

Name/Description: _____

_____ Rating: ☆☆☆☆☆

Name/Description: _____

_____ Rating: ☆☆☆☆☆

BEAN TO BONBON

Notes:

Share your feedback with us @ professorchocolate.com

GLOSSARY

Bonbon: A term stemming from the French word bon, meaning good. The term has come to represent a host of small confections, including a range of sugar and chocolate items.

Cacao bean (cocoa bean): The seed of the fruit of the tree, Theobroma cacao. The term cocoa is an anglicized version of the Latin cacao.

Caramel: Sugar that has been heated to around 340°F. Chemical reactions occur within the sugar molecule, producing a change in color and taste. The caramelized sugar can then be used to produce a wide range of confections from soft liquid centers to hard sucking candies.

Chocolate: A product of the bean of the cacao tree. Cocoa butter, cocoa liquor, sugar, flavoring (often vanilla), and an emulsifier (typically lecithin) are mixed to create chocolate.

Cocoa butter: The fat naturally present inside the cacao bean. It contains natural antioxidants and has a melting point which allows chocolate to literally melt in our mouths. White chocolate is produced by adding milk and sugar to cocoa butter.

Cocoa liquor: The dark liquid produced when cocoa beans are ground into a paste. Cocoa liquor has roughly equal parts cocoa solids and cocoa butter, but no alcohol. It is typically used to make unsweetened baking chocolate.

Ganache: A French term for a blended mixture of chocolate and a liquid (commonly heavy/double cream). Other liquids may be used to create vegan ganache variations. Often the addition of sugars, butter, and flavorings are used to enhance the taste of the ganache.

Gianduja: An Italian, nut-based confection consisting of nut pastes and chocolate. The most common version is a blend of hazelnuts and milk chocolate. The name is taken from a carnival character, Gianduja, who represents the typical Piedmontese. Piedmont is a region of Italy well-known for its hazelnut confections.

Liquor cordials: A liquid center confection made with a combination of sugar syrup and alcohol.

Marzipan: A nut-based confection typically made of cooked sugar and almonds blended into a paste.

Nougat: The French version of an aerated confection consisting of egg whites, cooked sugar, honey, nuts and sometimes dried fruit. The most well known version being Nougat Montélimar. The texture of nougat can vary from soft to very hard, with colors from white to dark brown. Similar confections can be found in other confectionary traditions as well, e.g. Spanish Turron, Italian Torroné and Persian Gaz. In the U.S. and England, nougat is most typically utilized as a filling in commercial candy bars, e.g. Milky Way and Three Musketeers.

Praline: A family of confections based on nuts coated in caramelized sugar. In chocolate shops, particularly Belgian ones, a praline is simply a filling surrounded by chocolate. In 1912, Jean Neuhaus made a chocolate shell, and filled it with almond paste,producing the first Belgian "praline".

Theobroma cacao: The Latin name for the tree bearing the cacao bean, from which chocolate is made.

Toffee: Different forms of candy are produced by melting sugar in water to produce syrup, and then heating. When syrup is mixed with butter and heated to a temperature of around 300º, the concentration of sugar reaches 99%, and toffee is formed. Fudge has a sugar content of about 85%, while caramel's content is 100%.

Truffle: A chocolate confection typically made of ganache that is piped or rolled into a ball and covered with chocolate and/or cocoa powder. The rough, earthy look of the cocoa powder is said to resemble the appearance of the truffle mushroom, hence the name.

—Damion Badalementi

PROFESSOR PICKS
Online Favorites

Here are some of our favorite chocolate-inspired places to visit online.

thechocolatelife.com

annmariekostyk.com

bellapinay.com

chocolateandzucchini.com

tcho.com

seventypercent.com

hotelchocolat.co.uk

zchocolat.com

chocolateobsession.com

rescuechocolate.com

echocolatenyc.com

Check professorchocolate.com for updates to this list

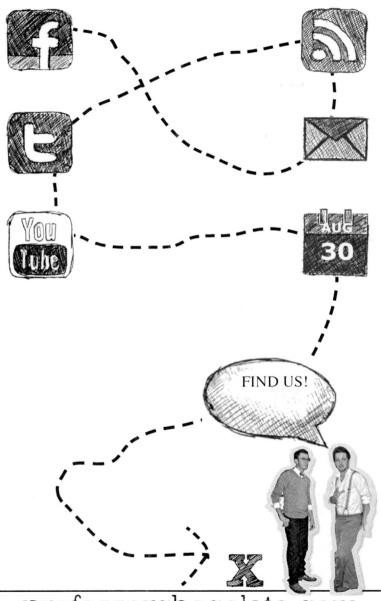

FIND US!

professorchocolate.com

ACKNOWLEDGEMENTS

We are forever indebted to a few individuals who helped make our dream of creating a chocolate handbook a reality. Without their dedication, effort, and late-night emails, this book would have been impossible to complete. Thank you!

Carlyn del Rosario & Elizabeth Doctors

First and foremost, we must thank the women in our lives. Carlyn and Liz have allowed us each to carry on this love affair with chocolate for quite some time. They've been exposed to, and have participated in, numerous conversations, planning sessions, and meetings. They have each played an integral (hands-on) role in the production of this book from start to finish, and of course, in supporting this dream of ours with relentless enthusiasm. Without the two of you, this book would still be a couple of journals and a large pile of loose papers.

Interior Design: Maura Gottstein (handpaintedinbrooklyn.com)

Taking hundreds of ideas, hand-drawn sketches, photos, napkins with notes on them, and verbal recommendations (and making sense of it all) requires a great deal of patience, and even more skill. We are indebted to Maura for helping us transition from talking about a chocolate book to actually producing one. Seeing our ideas brought to life has been a dream come true for us.

Cover Design/Web Design/Interior Design:
Rebecca Shotz (rebeccashotz.com) & Kurt Jeske (k.satellitegrp.com)

If we could write and produce a television series about a dynamic duo, all-encompassing, uber-talented design team, who travel around and save the day when projects start to go awry, it would certainly be based on Rebecca and Kurt. The only embellishment is that they travel around seeking publishers in distress. They are primarily based in Los Angeles. If you have design or production needs of any kind, they can certainly fulfill them.

Proofreading/Fact-Checking/Copy-Editing: Lauren Forgione

We truly didn't realize what an amazing job Lauren had done until we really started to make corrections based on her comments. She really went above and beyond what we expected and we look forward to working together on our next book! She did not look over certain segments of the book, so any visible mistakes are most certainly the fault of two absent-minded professors.

Proofreading: Carolyn Jervis Beitmann

Offering her time selflessly to proofread the many revisions we made to the profiles (plus the fact that Carolyn gave birth to Neill) means that we never could have accomplished this without her.
Thank you! We love you.

ABOUT THE PROFESSORS

Neill Alleva is a native of the Philadelphia suburbs and has been living in New York City since 2001. Neill's mother first introduced him to chocolate bonbons at an early age and has left an endearing impression. Since coming to NYC, he has been teaching elementary school children in Queens, NY. After work hours, Neill revels in foraging for all kinds of food, especially chocolate. He currently resides in Park Slope, Brooklyn, with his fiancé.

Rob Monahan is a fourth generation New Yorker. His grandmother, Rosemarie, worked for Barricini Candy for fifteen years, and passed on her confection affections to him. Rob has been teaching elementary school science for the past nine years and happily exploring Manhattan in search of chocolate for even longer. If he's not gormandizing at one of his favorite chocolate shops, you will probably find him at the nearest local cheese shop. He lives in Gramercy with his wife and son.

A portion of the profit from the sale of this book will be donated to two organizations that are near and dear to us.

As a survivor of childhood Leukemia, I attended this camp from 1988 to 1992. I returned as a volunteer counselor in 2007, one year before I was diagnosed with cholangiocarcinoma. From experience, I can say that this is a truly magical place for children who are suffering with serious illnesses. It is an honor to give something back to a place that has given so much to me. —Rob

The Hole in the Wall Gang Camp, started by Paul Newman over twenty years ago, provides children with cancer and other serious illnesses and conditions a camping experience of the highest quality, while extending year-round support to their families and health care providers.

The Hole in the Wall Gang Camp
565 Ashford Center Road
Ashford, CT 06278
860.429.3444 | holeinthewallgang.org

BARC is a not for profit animal shelter that has been run by caring animal lovers since 1987. Their mission is to create a loving, nurturing environment for abandoned animals until they can be placed in a permanent home. Check out barcshelter.org for more information on adoption or to volunteer.

Brooklyn Animal Resource Coalition (BARC)
253 Wythe Avenue
Williamsburg, Brooklyn
718.486.7489 | barcshelter.org